"Deliverance from the power of the evil one comes through definite resistance on the ground of the cross."

J.O. Fraser

(Abridged Edition)

By

Jessie Penn-Lewis

in collaboration with

Evan Roberts

CHRISTIAN • LITERATURE • CRUSADE
Fort Washington, Pennsylvania 19034

CHRISTIAN LITERATURE CRUSADE

U.S.A.
P.O. Box 1449, Fort Washington, PA 19034

GREAT BRITAIN
51 The Dean, Alresford, Hants., SO24 9BJ

AUSTRALIA
P.O. Box 91, Pennant Hills, N.S.W. 2120

NEW ZEALAND
P.O. Box 1203, Palmerston North

First American Edition 1977
Reprinted 1988

Revised & Reset by
CLC Editorial Team 1993

ISBN 0-87508-958-5

Originally published in England by
The Overcomer Literature Trust, Ltd.

Cover photo: Superstock

PRINTED IN THE UNITED STATES OF AMERICA

CONTENTS

Foreword 7
1. A Biblical Survey of Satanic Deception 11
2. The Satanic Confederacy of Wicked Spirits 35
3. Deception by Evil Spirits in Modern Times 55
4. The Perils of Passivity 75
5. Counterfeits of the Divine 97
6. Freedom for the Deceived 125
7. Volition and the Human Spirit 141
8. Victory in Conflict 159

APPENDIX

The Attitude of the Early Fathers to Evil Spirits 187
Symptoms of Demon Possession. Extracted from *Demon Possession*, by Dr. J. L. Nevius 188
Demoniacal Activity in Later Times. Sir Robert Anderson 190
The Physiology of the Spirit. From *Primeval Man Unveiled* 190
The Working of Evil Spirits in "Christian" Gatherings:
(1) Supposed conviction of sin by deceiving spirits .. 191
(2) Supposed unity for "revival" 193
(3) Supposed manifestations of the Holy Spirit 195
Light on "Abnormal" Experiences 197
How Demons Attack Advanced Believers 204
The True Workings of God, and Counterfeits of Satan 208

Unless otherwise noted, the Bible version quoted is the 1881 English Revised Version.

FOREWORD

JOHN WESLEY, in dealing with overbalance and fanaticism, uses the word *enthusiasm*, and says: "Enthusiasm is undoubtedly a disorder of the mind; and such disorder as greatly hinders the exercise of reason. Nay, sometimes it wholly sets it aside: it not only dims but shuts the eyes of the understanding. It may, therefore, well be accounted a species of madness; of madness rather than folly: seeing a fool is properly one who draws wrong conclusions from right premises; whereas a madman draws right conclusions, but from wrong premises. And so does an enthusiast. Suppose his premises are true, and his conclusions would necessarily follow. But here lies his mistake: *his premises are false*. He imagines himself to be what he is not, and therefore, *setting out wrong*, the farther he goes, the more he wanders out of the way."

Let us come nearer to our own time. I have on my shelves a book—*Group Movements of the Past and Experiments in Guidance*, by Ray Strachey—which consists of extracts from the papers of Hannah Whitall Smith, describing the times in which she lived, and the curious religious sects which she investigated during the middle years of the nineteenth century. In his foreword to this book, the late Dr. H. Hensley Henson, Bishop of Durham, wrote: "Very early in the history of the Christian Church the subtle temptation to a kind of inverted humility, which is really the worst and most dangerous form of spiritual pride, disclosed itself in portentous scandals. The adventists of Thessalonica, who refused their normal obligations in the interest of a complete self-preparation for the Lord's coming, have had their representatives in many strange sects in Europe and America, who have been carried into amazing extravagancies of creed and conduct. St. Paul's brusque judgment, 'If any will not work, neither let him eat' (2 Thessalonians 3:10), applies to them all. The ascetics of Colosse, whose punctilious rigorism coexisted with a perilous moral laxity, have had their successors in every Christian generation. Medieval monks and modern sectaries come together here. Both illustrate, in varying ways, the same spiritual malady. Such total prostration of the individual before the mandates of the divine Spirit seems to argue a genuine humility, but the implied assumption of plenary and direct personal inspiration discloses and fosters a spiritual arrogance none the less morally disintegrating because it is unsuspected. Experience has ever endorsed the great apostle's verdict. Over the whole woeful pageant of self-willed pietism, with its eccentric, arbitrary, even monstrous demands on its victims, the words may be written: '. . . which things have indeed a show of wisdom in will-worship, and humility, and severity to the body; but are not of any value against the indulgence of the flesh' (Colossians 2:23)."

An aftermath of the Welsh Revival at the dawn of the present century was the rise of a number of extreme cults, often stressing a return to "pentecostal" practices. Mrs. Penn-Lewis, who had witnessed much of the Revival as the representative of *The Life of Faith* magazine, saw clearly the peril of these fanatical teachings, and in collaboration with Mr. Evan Roberts, who played so prominent a part in the Revival, wrote a book, WAR ON THE SAINTS. In this book these extreme and overbalanced beliefs and practices are categorically branded as the work of an invading host of evil spirits. The word "*deception*" might be said to be the key word of the book—a term which is in complete harmony with the findings both of John Wesley and Dr. Henson.

This present volume is an abridgement of the original book, which ran into seven editions. The Trustees of The Overcomer Literature Trust were concerned about certain aspects of WAR ON THE SAINTS as originally published. First and foremost they felt that they could not endorse the teaching that a born-again, Spirit-filled Christian can at the same time be demon possessed; and they also found themselves unable to accept some of the teaching given concerning the "baptism of the Holy Spirit" and the aggressive warfare against the powers of darkness, either as a means of promoting revival or of hastening the coming again of the Lord Jesus Christ. As Editor of *The Overcomer* I was commissioned to undertake a revision of the book, with the object of eliminating these elements, and yet retaining the clear teaching and warning against the dangers underlying the extreme, unscriptural emphases of our modern array of "sects," behind which is so often hidden the clever manipulation of deceiving spirits. This has not been an easy task, and the result certainly will not satisfy everyone. But it is sent out with the prayer that the eyes of those who read it may be opened to the grave dangers that beset the path of uninformed "enthusiasm." Above all, may it give a new vision of the Mighty Saviour, who in His cross triumphed over all the powers of evil and deception and lives forever as the Strength and Refuge of His own.

J.C.Metcalfe

CHAPTER 1

A BIBLICAL SURVEY OF SATANIC DECEPTION

If all that the Bible contains on the subject of the supernatural powers of evil could be exhaustively dealt with in this book, we would find that more knowledge is given of the workings of Satan, and his principalities and powers, than many have realized. From Genesis to Revelation the work of Satan as deceiver of the whole inhabited earth can be traced until the climax is reached, and the full results of the deception in the Garden of Eden are unveiled in the Apocalypse. In Genesis we have the simple story of the garden, with the guileless pair unaware of danger from evil beings in the unseen world. We find recorded there Satan's first work as deceiver, and the subtle form of his method of deception. We see him working upon an innocent creature's highest and purest desires, and cloaking his own purpose of ruin under the guise of seeking to lead a human being nearer to God. We see him using the God-ward desires of Eve to bring about captivity and bondage to himself. We see him using "good" to bring about evil; suggesting evil to bring about supposed good. Caught with the bait of being "wise," and "like God," Eve is blinded to the principle involved in obedience to God, and is DECEIVED (1 Tim. 2:14, KJV).

Goodness is, therefore, no guarantee of protection from deception. The keenest way in which the devil deceives the world, and the Church, is when he comes in the guise of somebody, or something, which apparently causes them to go God-ward and good-ward. He said to Eve, "Ye shall be as gods," but he did not say, "and ye shall be like demons." Angels and men only knew evil when they fell into a state of evil. Satan did not tell Eve this when he added "knowing good *and evil*." His true objective in deceiving Eve was to get her to disobey God, but his wile was, "Ye shall be like God." Had she reasoned, she would have seen that the deceiver's suggestion exposed itself, for it crudely resolved itself into "disobey God" to be more like God!

The Curse of God Pronounced Upon the Deceiver

That a highly organized monarchy of evil spirit-beings was in existence is not made known in the story of the garden. Only a "serpent" is there; but the serpent is spoken to by God as an intelligent being, carrying out a deliberate purpose in the deception of the woman. The serpent-disguise of Satan is swept aside by Jehovah as He makes known the decision of the Triune God in view of the catastrophe which had taken place: a "Seed" of the deceived woman would eventually bruise the head of the supernatural being who had used the form of the serpent to carry out his plan. Yet from that point on the name of "serpent" is attached to him throughout the ages, for it describes the climax action of his revolt against his Creator in beguiling and deceiving the woman in Eden and blasting the human race. Satan triumphed, but God overruled. The victim is made the vehicle for the advent of a Victor, who would ultimately destroy the works of the devil and cleanse the heavens and the earth from every trace of his handiwork. The serpent is cursed, but, in effect, the beguiled victim is blessed, for through her will come the "Seed" which will triumph over the devil and his seed; and through her will arise a new race through the promised Seed (Gen. 3:15), a race which will be antagonistic to the serpent to the end of time, through the enmity implanted by God. Henceforth the story of the ages consists of the record of a war between these two seeds: the Seed of the woman—Christ and His redeemed—and the seed of the devil (See John 8:44; 1 John 3:10), right on to the furthermost point of the final committal of Satan to the lake of fire.

Henceforth it is also war by Satan upon the womanhood of the world, in malignant revenge for the verdict of the garden. Yes, war by the trampling down of women in all lands where the deceiver reigns. And war upon women in Christian lands too, by the continuance of his Eden method of misinterpreting the Word of God: insinuating into men's minds throughout all succeeding ages that God pronounced a "curse" upon the woman, when in truth she was pardoned and blessed; and instigating fallen men to personally carry out this supposed curse, though in truth it was a CURSE UPON THE DECEIVER and not upon the deceived one (Gen. 3:14).

"I will put enmity between *thee* and the woman," said God, as well as between "*thy* seed and her seed," and this vindictive enmity of the hierarchy of evil toward women, and especially believers, has not lessened in its intensity from that day.

Satan as Deceiver in the Old Testament

When once we clearly recognize the existence of an unseen host of evil spirit-beings, all actively engaged in deceiving and misleading humans, Old Testament history will convey to us an open vision of their doings otherwise hidden from our knowledge. We can trace their operations in relation to the servants of God throughout all history and discern the work of Satan as deceiver penetrating everywhere. We shall see that David was deceived by Satan into numbering Israel because he failed to recognize that the suggestion to his mind was from a satanic source (1 Chron. 21:1). Job also was deceived, as were the messengers that came to him, when he believed the report that the fire which had fallen from heaven was "from God" (Job 1:16), and that all the other calamities which befell him in the loss of wealth, home and children came directly from the hand of God. For the early part of the book of Job clearly shows that Satan was the primary cause of all his troubles as "prince of the power of the air," using the elements of nature and the wickedness of men to afflict the servant of God. He hoped that ultimately he could force Job into renouncing his faith in God, who seemed to be unjustly punishing him without cause. That this was Satan's aim is suggested in the words of the wife of the patriarch, who became a tool for the Adversary when she urged the suffering man to "curse God and die." She also was deceived by the Enemy into believing that God was the primary cause of all the trouble and the unmerited suffering which had come upon him.

In the history of Israel during the time of Moses, the veil is lifted more clearly from the satanic powers and we are shown the condition of the world as sunk in idolatry—said in the New Testament to be the direct work of Satan (1 Cor. 10:20)—and having actual dealing with evil spirits. The whole inhabited earth was thus in a state of deception and held by the deceiver in his power. We also find numbers of the people of Israel, through contact with others under satanic power, deceived into communicating with "familiar spirits" and into the using of "divination" and other kindred arts inculcated by the powers of darkness—even though they knew the laws of God and had seen His manifested judgments among them (see Lev. 17:7, margin: "*satyrs*"; 19:31; 20:6, 27; Deut. 18:10–11).

In the book of Daniel we find a still further stage of

revelation reached concerning the hierarchy of evil powers when, in the tenth chapter, we are shown the existence of two "princes" of Satan actively opposing the messenger of God sent to Daniel to make him understand God's counsels for His people. There are also other references to the workings of Satan, his princes, and the hosts of wicked spirits carrying out his will, scattered throughout the Old Testament; but on the whole the veil is kept upon their doings until the great hour arrives when the "Seed" of the woman, who was to bruise the head of the serpent, is manifested on earth in human form (Gal. 4:4).

Satan as Deceiver Unveiled in the New Testament

With the advent of Christ, the veil which had hidden the active workings of the supernatural powers of evil for centuries since the garden catastrophe is still further removed, and their deception and power over man is clearly revealed. The arch-deceiver himself appears in the wilderness conflict with the Lord to challenge the "Seed of the woman"—in a way not recorded since he appeared on earth at the time of the Fall. So the wilderness of Judea and the Garden of Eden become parallel arenas for the testing of the first and the Second Adam. In both encounters Satan worked as deceiver, but in the second instance he wholly failed to deceive and beguile the One who had come as his Conqueror.

Traces of the characteristic work of Satan as deceiver can be discerned also among the disciples of Christ. The devil deceives Peter into speaking words of temptation to the Lord, suggesting His turning from the path of the cross (Matt. 16:22–23). Later on he takes hold of the same disciple in the Judgment Hall (Luke 22:31), prompting him to declare "I know not the man," with the hope of camouflage (Matt. 26:74). Further traces of the work of the deceiver may be seen in the epistles of Paul: in his references to "false apostles," "deceitful workers," and Satan's workings as an "angel of light" promoting "his ministers as ministers of righteousness" among the people of God (2 Cor. 11:13–15). Again in the messages to the seven Asian churches, given by the ascended Lord to His servant John, false apostles are spoken of, and false teachings of many kinds. A "synagogue of Satan" (Rev. 2:9), consisting of deceived ones at Smyrna, is mentioned, and "deep things of Satan" are described as existing in the church at Thyatira (Rev. 2:24).

THE REVELATION OF THE DECEIVER IN THE APOCALYPSE

A startling revelation of the satanic confederacy against God and His Christ is given to the Apostle John. After the messages to the seven churches, the world-wide work of the deceiver-prince is fully disclosed to the apostle. He is bidden to write all that he is shown, so that the Church of Christ might know the full meaning of the war with Satan in which the redeemed would be engaged right on to the time when the Lord Jesus would be revealed from heaven in judgment upon these vast and terrible powers—powers which are full of cunning malignity and hatred to His people, and truly at work behind the world of men from the days of the garden story to the end.

As we read the Apocalypse it is important to remember that even though the organized forces of Satan described there were in existence at the time of the Fall in Eden, they were only partially revealed to the people of God prior to the advent of the promised "Seed of the woman" who was to bruise the serpent's head. When the fullness of time came, God manifest in the flesh met the fallen archangel, the leader of the evil angelic hosts, in mortal combat at Calvary. Putting them to open shame, He shook off from Himself vast masses of the hosts of darkness who had gathered around the cross from the furthermost realms of the kingdom of Satan (Col. 2:15).

The Scriptures teach us that God's unveilings of the truths concerning Himself, and of all the things in the spiritual realm which we need to know, are always timed by Him to match the strength of His people. The full revelation of these satanic powers disclosed in the Apocalypse was not given to the Church in its infancy—some forty years passed after the Lord's ascension before the Book of Revelation was written. Possibly it was necessary that the Church of Christ should first fully grasp the fundamental truths revealed to Paul and the other apostles before she could safely be shown the extent of the war with supernatural powers of evil upon which she had entered.

In the vision given to John, the name and character of the deceiver is more clearly made known, along with the strength of his forces and the extent of the war and its final issues. It is shown that in the invisible realm there is war between the forces of evil and the forces of light. John says that "the dragon WARRED, and his angels" (Rev. 12:7), the dragon being explicitly described as the "old serpent, called the Devil and Satan," the deceiver of the whole inhabited earth. His world-wide work as deceiver is fully revealed, and the war in the earth-realm caused by his deceiving of the races and the world powers acting under his instigation and rule. The highly organized confederacy of principalities and powers acknowledging the headship of Satan is disclosed, and their "authority over every tribe and people and tongue and nation," all deceived by the supernatural and invisible forces of evil, and making "war with the saints" (Rev. 13:7).

World-wide Deception Disclosed in the Apocalypse

War is the key word of the Apocalypse: war on a

scale undreamed of by mortal man; war between vast angelic powers of light and darkness; war by the dragon and the deceived world powers upon the saints; war by the same world powers against the Lamb; war by the dragon upon the Church; war in many phases and forms, until the end when the Lamb overcomes, and they also overcome who are with Him, "called and chosen and faithful" (Rev. 17:14).

The world is now drawing nearer to "the time of the end," characterized by the deception depicted in the Apocalypse as being world-wide—when there will be deception both of nations and individuals, on such a vast scale that the deceiver will practically have the whole earth under his control. Before this climax is reached, there will be preliminary stages of the deceiver's working, marked by the widespread deception of individuals both within and outside of the professing Church—beyond the ordinary condition of deception in which the unregenerate world is lying.

To understand why the deceiver will be able to produce this world-wide deception which will permit the supernatural powers to carry out their will and drive nations and men into active rebellion against God, we need clearly to grasp what the Scriptures say about unregenerate men in their normal condition, and the world in its fallen state.

If Satan is described in the Apocalypse as the deceiver of the whole earth, he has been so from the beginning. "The whole world lieth in the evil one" (1 John 5:19), said the apostle to whom was given the Revelation, describing the world as already lying deep in darkness through the deception of the evil one and blindly led by him through vast evil spirit hosts under his control.

The Word "Deceived"
The Description of Every Unregenerate Man

The word "deceived" is, according to the Scripture,

the description of every unregenerate human being, without distinction of person, race, culture, or sex. "We also were . . . deceived" (Titus 3:3), said Paul the Apostle, although in his "deceived" condition he had been a religious man, "walking according to the righteousness of the law, blameless" (Phil. 3:6).

Every unregenerate man is first of all deceived by his own deceitful heart (Jer. 17:9; Isa. 44:20) and by sin (Heb. 3:13). Then the god of this world adds the "blinding of the mind," lest the light of the gospel of Christ should dispel the darkness (2 Cor. 4:4). Nor does the deception of the evil one wholly end when the regenerating life of God reaches the person, for this blinding of the mind is removed only so far as the deceptive lies of Satan are dislodged by the light of truth.

Even though the heart is renewed and the will has turned to God, the deeply ingrained disposition to self-deception remains. This power of the deceiver to blind the mind betrays itself in many forms, as the following statements from Scripture show:

The man is *deceived* if he is a hearer but not a doer of the Word of God (Jas. 1:22).

He is *deceived* if he says he has no sin (1 John 1:8).

He is *deceived* when he thinks himself to be "something" when he is nothing (Gal. 6:3).

He is *deceived* when he thinks himself to be wise with the wisdom of this world (1 Cor. 3:18).

He is *deceived* by seeming to be religious when an unbridled tongue reveals his true condition (Jas. 1:26).

He is *deceived* if he thinks he can sow and not reap what he sows (Gal. 6:7).

He is *deceived* if he thinks the unrighteous will inherit the kingdom of God (1 Cor. 6:9).

He is *deceived* if he thinks that contact with sin will not have its effect upon him (1 Cor. 15:33).

DECEIVED! How the word repels, and how involuntarily every human being resents it as applied to himself—not realizing that the very repulsion is the work of the deceiver for the purpose of keeping the deceived ones from knowing the truth and being set free from deception. If men can be so easily fooled by the deception arising from their own fallen nature, surely the forces of Satan will eagerly seek to add to it and not diminish it by one iota. How keenly will they work to keep men in bondage to the old creation. How multitudinous are the forms of self-deception, enabling them the more readily to carry on their deceiving work! Their methods of deception are old and new, adapted to suit the nature, state and circumstances of the victim. Impelled by malice and ill-will towards mankind and hatred of all goodness, the emissaries of Satan do not fail to execute their plans, persevering to reach their goal.

SATAN, THE DECEIVER ALSO OF THE CHILDREN OF GOD

Yes, the arch-deceiver is not only the deceiver of the whole unregenerate world but of the children of God also, with this basic difference: that in the deception he seeks to practice upon the saints he changes his tactics. He works with acutest strategy, in wiles of error and deception concerning the things of God (Matt. 24:24; 2 Cor. 11:3, 13–15).

The chief weapon which the deceiver-prince of darkness relies upon to keep the world in his power is deception, but it appears in varying guises. Being no fool, Satan contrives to beguile each person in a way appropriate to the particular stage of his spiritual life. There is: (1) deception for the unregenerate, who are already held by sin; (2) deception suited to the carnal Christian; (3) and deception fitted to the spiritual believer. When one passes out of a preceding stage, he must expect more subtle temptations than before. He may be fully able to recognize the earlier forms of deception for what they are, and thereby overcome them, but he should be aware that the closer one is to God, the more sly and cunning Satan's seductions are likely to be.

Let the deception be removed which held the man in the days of his unregenerate condition, and in the days of his carnal Christian life; when he emerges into the heavenly places, described by Paul in the Epistle to the Ephesians, he will find himself showered upon and buffeted by some of the keenest workings of the deceiver, for the deceiving spirits are actively at work attacking those who are united to the risen Lord.

The work of the deceiver among the saints of God is especially depicted in the Ephesian letter of the Apostle Paul, where, in chapter 6:10–18, we have the veil drawn aside from the satanic powers, showing their war upon the Church of God, and the individual believer's armor and weapons for conquering the foe. From this passage we learn that in the plane of the believer's highest experience of union with the Lord, and in the "high places" of the spiritual maturity of the Church, will the keenest and closest battle be fought with the deceiver and his hosts.

A glimpse into this onslaught of deceiving spirits upon the people of God at the close of the age is given in the Gospel of Matthew, where the Lord uses the word *deceive* in describing some of the special marks of the latter days. He said: "Take heed that no man deceive you. For many shall come in My name, saying, 'I am the Christ'; and shall lead many astray" (Matt. 24:4–5); "And many false prophets shall arise, and shall deceive many" (Matt. 24:11, KJV); "There shall arise false Christs, and false prophets, and shall show great signs and wonders, so as to lead astray [or "deceive," KJV], if possible, even the elect" (Matt. 24:24).

Deception in Connection with the Supernatural Realm

This special form of deception is pointedly said to be

in connection with *spiritual* rather than worldly things. This surely shows that the people of God, at the time of the end, will be expecting the coming of the Lord, and we can infer that they will be *keenly awake to all movements from the supernatural world,* in such a measure that deceiving spirits will be able to take advantage of it and anticipate the Lord's appearing by "false Christs" and false signs and wonders. They will mix their counterfeits with the true manifestations of the Spirit of God. The Lord says that men will be deceived (1) concerning Christ and His *parousia* (appearing); (2) concerning *prophecy*—teachings regarding the future, from the spiritual world through inspired messengers; and (3) concerning the *giving of proofs* that the "teachings" are truly of God, by "signs" and "wonders" so Godlike as to be indistinguishable from the true even by those described as "the elect"—who will need to possess some other test than the judging by appearances of a "sign" being from God if they are to be able to discern the false from the true.

The Apostle Paul's words to Timothy, containing the special prophecy given to him by the Holy Spirit for the Church of Christ in the last days of the dispensation, exactly coincide with the words of the Lord recorded by Matthew. These two letters of Paul to Timothy are the last epistles that he wrote before his departure to be with Christ. Both were written in prison, and Paul's prison was to him what Patmos was to John—a time when he was "in the Spirit" (Rev. 1:10) and shown things to come. Paul was giving his last directions to Timothy for the ordering of the Church of God right on to the end of her time on earth—giving rules to guide not only Timothy but all God's servants "in dealing with God's household." In the midst of all these detailed instructions, his keen seer's vision looks on to the "later times"; and by express command of the Spirit of God he depicts in a few brief sentences the peril of the Church in those times, in the same way that the Spirit of God gave the prophets of the Old Testament some pregnant prophecy only to be fully understood after the events had come to pass.

The apostle said: "The Spirit saith expressly, that in later times some shall fall away from the faith, giving heed to seducing spirits and doctrines of demons, through the hypocrisy of men that speak lies, seared in their own conscience as with a hot iron . . ." (1 Tim. 4:1–2, mg.).

Paul's Statement in 1 Timothy 4:1–3 Is the Only Specific One Showing the Cause of the Peril

Paul's prophetic statement appears to be all that is foretold in specific words about the Church and its history in "later times." The Lord Jesus spoke in general terms about the dangers which would encompass His people at the time of the end, and Paul wrote to the Thessalonians more fully about the apostasy and the wicked deceptions of the lawless one in the last days, but the passage in Timothy is the only one which explicitly shows the special cause of the peril of the Church in its closing days on earth, and how the wicked spirits of Satan would break in upon her members and by *deception* beguile some away from their purity of faith in Christ.

The Holy Spirit, in this brief message given to Paul, describes the character and work of the evil spirits so that we might recognize (1) their *existence*, and (2) their efforts directed *towards believers* to *deceive* them and draw them away from the path of simple faith in Christ—all that is included in "the faith which was once for all delivered unto the saints" (Jude 3).

That the character of the *spirits* is described in 1 Timothy 4:1–3 and not the men they sometimes use in the work of deception, may be understood from the Greek original.*

The peril of the Church at the close of the age is therefore from supernatural beings who are "hypocrites"—who pretend to be what they are not—who give "teachings" which appear to make for greater holiness by producing ascetic severity to the "flesh," but who themselves are wicked and unclean and bring those they deceive into contact with the foulness of their own presence.

The Peril of Deceiving Spirits Affects Every Child of God

This peril concerns every professing Christian. The prophecy of the Holy Spirit declares that (1) "*some*" shall fall away from the faith. (2) The reason for the fall will be a "*giving heed to seducing spirits.*" The nature of this working is not the promotion of obvious evil, but deception, which is a covert working. The essence of deception is that the operation is looked upon as sincere and pure. (3) The nature of the deception will be in *doctrines* of demons, *i.e.*, the deception will be in a doctrinal sphere. (4) The way of deception will be that the "doctrines" are delivered with "hypocrisy," *i.e.*, spoken as if *true*. (5) Two instances of the effect of these evil spirit doctrines are given: (*a*) the forbidding of marriage, and (*b*) abstaining from meats. But both of these common activities—marrying and the eating of meat—are, said Paul, divinely ordained—"created by God." Therefore their prohibition is a mark of opposition to God, even in His work as Creator.

---

* Pember says that verse 2 refers to the *character* of the deceiving spirits and should be read thus: ". . . direct teaching of unclean spirits, who, though bearing a brand on their own conscience—as a criminal is disfigured—would pretend to sanctity [*i.e.*, holiness] to gain credence for their lies. . . ."

The Satanic Forces Described in Ephesians 6

Demoniacal "doctrines" have been generally calculated as either belonging to the Church of Rome—because of the two specific results of demon teaching mentioned by Paul which characterize that Church—or to later "cults" and skewed "movements" of the twentieth century, with their omission of the fact of sin and the need of the atoning sacrifice of Christ, the divine Saviour. But there is a vast realm of doctrinal deception by deceiving spirits penetrating and interpenetrating evangelical Christendom also. Yes, evil spirits, in more or less degree, influence the lives even of Christian men, and bring them under their power. Even spiritual Christians can be thus affected on the plane described by the apostle, where believers united to the risen Christ meet "spiritual wickedness" in "heavenly places." For the satanic forces described in Ephesians 6:12 are shown to be divided into (1) "*Principalities*"—demonic officers dealing with nations and governments; (2) "*Powers*"—those having authority and power of action in certain special spheres open to them; (3) "*World-rulers*"—spirits governing the darkness and blindness of the world at large. All of these are wicked spirits operating from *celestial realms*, directing their forces against the Church of Jesus Christ, using "wiles," "fiery darts," sly onslaughts, and every conceivable deception about "doctrines" which they are capable of planning.

This peril assails the Church from the *supernatural* world. It comes from supernatural spirit-beings who are persons (Mark 1:25) having the power of intelligence to plan (Matt. 12:44–45) and devise strategy (Eph. 6:11), resulting in the deception of those who "give heed" to them.

HOW EVIL SPIRITS DECEIVE BY "DOCTRINES"

Why are evil spirits able to get men to receive their teachings? There are three basic reasons:

(1) Some people naively believe that anything supernatural has its source in God: occult forces do not exist. Any spiritual revelation or teaching is assumed to be divine because it is supernatural. Any "flash of light" on a text, any "vision of Christ" or of an "angelic being" is considered as sent by the Holy Spirit. The possibility of deception from a demonic source is never given thought. Such persons, obviously, are wide open to arcane doctrines—even if they should be Christians.

(2) Most Christians, however, would be greatly surprised to have an explicitly supernatural experience—a vision or some other paranormal revelation. Though they believe that both God and Satan exist, and angels and demons also, a direct encounter with any of them would be considered abnormal and possibly suspect. So with these less gullible persons deceiving spirits will normally take a more subtle approach. They will attempt to mix their "teachings" with the man's own reasonings, so that he thinks he has come to his own conclusions on the matter under consideration. The teachings of the deceiving spirits in this form are so natural in appearance that they seem to come from the man himself as the fruit of his own mind and reasoning. The spirits counterfeit the working of the human brain, and inject thoughts and suggestions into the human mind; for they can directly communicate with the mind, quite apart from gaining possession (in any degree) of mind or body.

Those who are thus deceived believe that they have come to their own conclusions by their own reasonings, ignorant that the deceiving spirits have incited them to "reason" *without sufficient data, or on a wrong premise,* and thus come to false conclusions. The teaching spirit has achieved his own end by putting a lie in the man's mind, through the instrumentality of a false reasoning.

(3) But perhaps even more common is the indirect means: by the use of deceived human teachers, supposedly conveying undiluted divine truth—instructors who are implicitly believed because of their godly life and character. The trustful student says, "He is a good man, even a *holy* man, and I believe him." The life of the man is taken as a sufficient guarantee for his teaching, instead of judging the teaching by the Scriptures, apart from his personal character. This has its foundation in the prevalent idea that everything that Satan and his evil spirits do is *manifestly* evil, the truth not being recogized that they work under cover of light (2 Cor. 11:14). If demons can get a "good man" to accept some idea from them, and pass it on as "truth," he is a better instrument for deceptive purposes than a bad man who would not be believed.

False and Deceived Teachers

There is a difference between "false" teachers and *deceived* ones. There are many deceived ones among the most able teachers today because they do not recognize that an army of teaching spirits have come forth to deceive the people of God and that the special peril of the earnest section of the professing Church lies in the supernatural realm, from whence the deceiving spirits with "teachings" are whispering their lies to all who are "spiritual," *i.e.*, open to spiritual things. These "teaching spirits" with "doctrines" will make a special effort to deceive those who have to transmit doctrine and seek to mingle their teachings with truth so as to get them accepted. Every believer must test all teachers today for himself, by the Word of God and by their attitude to the atoning cross of Christ and other fundamental truths of the gospel, and not be misled into testing "teaching" by the character of the teacher. Good men can be deceived, and Satan needs good men to float his lies under the guise of truth.

THE EFFECT ON THE CONSCIENCE OF THE TEACHINGS BY EVIL SPIRITS

How teaching spirits teach we find described by Paul, for he says they speak lies in *hypocrisy*, that is, speak lies as if they were truth. And the effect of their working is said to "cauterize" (Gr.) the conscience; *i.e.*, if a man accepts the teachings of evil spirits as divine, because they come to him "supernaturally," and he obeys and follows those teachings, conscience is *unused*, so that it practically becomes dulled and passive—or seared. And a man will do things under the influence of supernatural "revelation" which an actively awakened conscience would keenly rebuke and condemn. Such people "give heed" to these spirits, by (1) *listening* to them, and then by (2) *obeying* them; for they are deceived by accepting wrong thoughts about God's presence, and about divine love, and unknowingly give themselves up to the power of lying spirits. Working in the line of "teaching," deceiving spirits will insert their lies spoken in *hypocrisy* into "holiness" teaching and deceive believers about sin, themselves, and all other truths connected with the spiritual life.

Scripture is generally used as the basis of these teachings and is skillfully woven together like a spider's web, so that the listeners are caught in the snare. Single texts are wrenched from their context, and from their place in the perspective of truth; sentences are taken from their correlative sentences, or texts are aptly picked out from over a wide field and so netted together as to appear to give a full revelation of the mind of God—but the intervening passages, giving historical setting, actions and circumstances connected with the speaking of the words, and other elements which give light on each separate text, are skillfully dropped out.

A wide net is thus made for the unwary or the untaught in the principles of Scripture exegesis, and many a life is sidetracked and troubled by this false use of the Word of God. Because the experience of most professing Christians in regard to the devil is limited to knowing him as a tempter, or as an accuser, they have no concept of the depths of his wickedness and of the wickedness of evil spirits, and are under the impression that they will not quote Scripture, whereas they will quote the whole Book if they can but deceive one soul.

Some Ways of "Teaching" by Deceiving Spirits

The "teachings" of deceiving spirits now being promulgated by them are too many in number to enumerate in a small compass. They are generally recognized only in "false religions," but the teaching spirits with their "doctrines" or religious ideas suggested to the minds of men are ceaselessly at work in every clime, seeking to play upon the religious instinct in men and give a substitute for truth.

Therefore, truth alone dispels the deceptive doctrines of the teaching spirits of Satan—the truth of God, not merely "views of truth": truth concerning all the principles and laws of the God of Truth. "Doctrines of demons" simply consist of that which a man "thinks" and "believes" as the outcome of suggestions made to his mind by deceiving spirits. All "thought" and "belief" belongs to one of two realms: the realm of truth, or the realm of falsehood—each having its source in God or Satan. All truth comes from God, and all that is contrary to truth is from Satan. Even the "thoughts" that apparently originate in a man's own mind come from one of these two sources, for the mind itself is either darkened by Satan (2 Cor. 4:4) and therefore fertile soil for his "teachings," or is renewed by God (Eph. 4:23) and hence clarified from the veil of Satan and made open to the reception and transmission of truth.

THE BASIC PRINCIPLE FOR TESTING TEACHINGS BY TEACHING SPIRITS

Since thought, or "belief," originates either from the God of Truth or the father of lies (John 8:44), there is but one basic principle for testing the source of all doctrines and philosophical beliefs held by believers or unbelievers, *i.e.*, the test of the revealed Word of God.

All genuine "truth" is in harmony with the only channel of revealed truth in the world—the written Word of God. On the other hand, all teachings originating from deceiving spirits:

(1) Weaken the authority of the Scriptures;
(2) Distort the teaching in the Scriptures;
(3) Add to the Scriptures the thoughts of men; or
(4) Put the Scriptures entirely aside.

The ultimate object of the forces of falsehood is to hide, distort, misuse or put aside the revelation of God concerning the cross of Calvary, where Satan was overthrown by the God-Man and where freedom was obtained for all his captives.

The *test* of all religious belief therefore is:

(1) Its harmony with the written Scriptures in its full body of truth.
(2) Its attitude toward the cross and sin.

In the Christianized world some doctrines of demons, *tested by these two primary principles*, may be mentioned:

Christian Science __ no *sin*, no Saviour, no cross.
Theosophy ________ no *sin*, no Saviour, no cross.
Spiritism__________ no *sin*, no Saviour, no cross.
New Theology _____ no *sin*, no Saviour, no cross.

In the heathen world:

1.	Islam, Confucianism, Buddhism, etc.	No Saviour, no cross, a "moral" religion with man his own saviour.
2.	Idolatry as the worship of demons.	No knowledge of a Saviour, or of His Calvary sacrifice, but true knowledge of the evil powers, which they endeavor to propitiate, because they have proved them to be existent.

In the professing Christian Church: Countless concepts and beliefs which are opposed to the truth of God are injected into the minds of "Christians" by teaching spirits, rendering them ineffective in the warfare with sin and Satan and subject to the power of evil spirits. All new insights and systems of belief should therefore be tested by the truth of God revealed in the Scripture, not merely by texts or portions of the Word but by the principles of truth revealed in the Word. Since Satan will endorse his teachings by "signs and wonders" (Matt. 24:24; 2 Thess. 2:9; Rev. 13:13), "fire from heaven" and other supernatural "signs" are no proof of a teaching being of God; nor is a "beautiful life" to be the infallible test, for even Satan's ministers can be "ministers of righteousness" (2 Cor. 11:13–15).

The Culmination of the Floodtide of Deceiving Spirits Shown in 2 Thessalonians 2

The culmination of the rising tide of these deceiving spirits sweeping upon the Church is described by the Apostle Paul in his second letter to the Thessalonians, where he speaks of the manifestation of someone who will, eventually, have so deceived Christendom as to have gained an entrance into the very sanctuary of

God; so that "he sitteth in the sanctuary of God, setting himself forth as God. . . ." The bearing of this one will be a "presence" like God, and yet "according to the working of Satan, with all power, and signs, and wonders of falsehood, and with all deceit . . ." (2 Thess. 2:4, 9–10, mg.).

Confirmation of our Lord's words recorded by Matthew is found in the revelation given by Him to John on Patmos, that at the close of the age the main weapon used by the deceiver for obtaining power over the people of the earth will be supernatural signs from heaven, when a counterfeit "lamb" will do "great signs," and *even "make fire come down out of heaven"* to deceive the dwellers on the earth, thereby exercising such control over the whole world that "no man shall be able to buy or sell, save he that hath the mark of the beast" (Rev. 13:11–17). Through this supernatural deception, the full purpose of the deceiving hierarchy of Satan reaches its consummation in the foretold world-wide authority.

Deception of the world with deepening darkness, including deception of the Church through arcane "teachings" and "manifestations," will reach the highest floodtide climax at the close of the age. It is striking to note that John, the apostle who was chosen to transmit the Apocalypse to the Church in preparation for the last days of the Church militant, should be the one who wrote to the Christians of his day, "Believe not every spirit . . ." (1 John 4:1–6). He earnestly warned his "children" that the "spirit of antichrist" and the "spirit of error" (deception) was already actively at work among them. Their attitude was to be "believe not"—*i.e.*, to doubt every supernatural teaching and teacher *until proved to be of God.* They were to *prove* the "teachings," lest they came from a "spirit of error" and were part of the deceiver's campaign as "antichrist," *i.e., against Christ.*

If this attitude of neutrality and doubt toward supernatural teachings was needed in the days of the Apostle John—some fifty-seven years after Pentecost—how much more is it needed in the "later times" foretold by the Lord, and by the Apostle Paul. Times which were to be characterized by a clamor of voices of "prophets": that is—in the language of the twentieth century—"speakers" and "teachers" using the sacred name of the Lord; and when "teachings" received supernaturally from the spiritual realm would abound—"teachings" accompanied with such wonderful proofs of their "divine" origin as to perplex even the most faithful of the Lord's people, and even, for a time, to DECEIVE some of them.

OUTWARD SUCCESS OR DEFEAT NO TRUE CRITERION FOR JUDGMENT

The enemy is a deceiver, and as a deceiver he will work and prevail in the later times. "Success" or "defeat" is no criterion of a work being of God or Satan. Calvary stands forever as the revelation of God's way in working out His redemptive purposes. Satan works for *time*, for he knows his time is short, but God works for *eternity*. Through death to life, through defeat to triumph, through suffering to joy—this is God's way.

Knowledge of truth is the primary safeguard against deception. The "elect" must *know*, and they must learn to test and "prove the spirits" *until they do know* what is of God and what is of Satan. The words of the Master, "Take heed, *I have told you*," plainly imply that personal knowledge of danger is part of the Lord's way of guarding His own. Those who blindly rely upon "the keeping power of God" without seeking to understand how to escape deception, when forewarned to "take heed" by the Lord, will surely find themselves entrapped by the subtle foe.

CHAPTER 2

The Satanic Confederacy of Wicked Spirits

A perspective view of the ages covered by the history given in Bible records shows that the rise in spiritual power of the people of God was marked by the recognition of the existence of demoniacal hosts of evil. When the Church of God in the old and new dispensations was at the highest point of spiritual power, its leaders recognized, and drastically dealt with, the invisible forces of Satan; and when it was at the lowest, they were ignored or allowed to have free course among the people.

God Legislating for Dangers From Evil Spirits

The reality of the existence of wicked spirits by whom Satan, their prince, carries out his work in the fallen world of men cannot be more strongly proved than by the fact that the statutes given by Jehovah to Moses on the fiery mount embodied stringent measures for dealing with the attempts of evil spirit-beings to gain power over the people of God. Moses was instructed by Jehovah to keep the camp of Israel free from their inroads by the drastic penalty of death for all who had dealings with them (Lev. 20:27). The very fact of Jehovah thus giving statutes in connection with such a subject, and the extreme penalty to be enforced for disobedience to His law, shows in itself (1) the existence of evil spirits, (2) their wickedness, (3) their ability to communicate with and influence human beings, and (4) the necessity for uncompromising hostility to them and their works. God would not legislate about dangers which had no real existence, nor would He command the extreme penalty of death if the contact of people with evil spirit-beings of the unseen world did not necessitate such drastic dealing.

The severity of the penalty obviously implies, also, that the leaders of Israel must have been given acute ability for "discerning of spirits," so sure and so clear that they could have no doubt in deciding cases brought before them.

While Moses and Joshua lived and enforced the strong measures decreed by God to keep His people free from the inroads of satanic power, Israel remained in allegiance to God—at the highest point of its history; but when these leaders died, the nation sank into darkness, brought about by evil spirit-powers drawing the people into idolatry and sin. The condition of the nation in later years rose or fell because of (1) allegiance to God, or (2) idolatrous worship of spirits (see Judges 2:19, 1 Kings 14:22–24; compare 2 Chron. 33:1–5, 34:1–7), and all the sins resulting therefrom. For what actually is idolatry but the worship of demons in place of Jehovah (1 Corinthians 10:20).

When the new dispensation opens with the advent of Christ, we find the God-Man recognizing the existence of the satanic powers of evil and manifesting uncompromising hostility toward them and their works. As with Moses in the Old Testament, so was the abhorrence by Christ in the New. Moses was the man who knew God face to face; Christ was the Only Begotten Son of the Father, sent expressly from God to the world of men. And each definitely recognized the existence of Satan and other evil spirit-beings; each drastically dealt with them as entering and possessing men; and each waged war against them, as actively opposed to God.

Taking a perspective view, from the time of Christ on throughout the early history of the Church and up to the giving of the Apocalypse and the death of the Apostle John, the manifested power of God worked among His people, and the leaders recognized and dealt with the spirits of evil. This period corresponded to the Mosaic period in the old dispensation.

CHRISTENDOM IN THE MIDDLE AGES

In the post-apostolic period this manifested power of God continued in varying degrees, rising and subsiding. Then the forces of darkness gained, and, with intermittent intervals and exceptions, the professing Church sank down under their power, until, in the darkest hour, which we call the Middle Ages, sins having their rise through the deceptive workings of the evil spirits of Satan were as rife as in Canaan before its conquest. Moses had written by the command of God: "Thou shalt not learn to do after the abominations of those nations. There shall not be found with thee . . . one that useth divination, or that practiceth augury, or an enchanter, or a sorcerer, or a charmer, or a consulter with a familiar spirit, or a wizard, or a necromancer" (Deut. 18:9–11). But even as in Old Testament times, this admonition was again often ignored.

CHRISTENDOM IN THE PRESENT CENTURY

Why Christendom in the present century does not universally recognize the existence and workings of evil supernatural forces can only be attributed to its low condition of spiritual life and power. Even at the present time, when the existence of evil spirits is recognized by the heathen, this is often looked upon by the Western missionary as "superstition" and ignorance. Actually, such ignorance is on the part of the shepherd who is blinded by the prince of the power of the air to the revelation given in the Scriptures concerning these satanic powers.

The "ignorance" on the part of the heathen is in their *propitiatory* attitude to evil spirits. They seek to *appease* the spirits because of their ignorance of the gospel message of a Deliverer and Saviour sent to "proclaim release to the captives" (Luke 4:18), and who, when He was on earth, went about healing all who were "oppressed by the devil" (Acts 10:38). He also sent His messengers to open the eyes of the bound ones, that they might "turn from darkness to light, and from the power of Satan unto God" (Acts 26:18).

If missionaries to the heathen recognized the existence of evil spirits, and that the darkness in heathen lands was caused by the prince of the power of the air (Eph. 2:2; 4:18; 1 John 5:19; 2 Cor. 4:4), and then proclaimed to the heathen the message of deliverance from the evil hosts they know so well to be real and malignant foes—this in addition to the remission of sins and victory over sin through the atoning sacrifice of Calvary—a vast change would come over the mission field in a few brief years.

Believers May Receive Equipment to Deal with Satanic Powers

The hour of need always brings a corresponding measure of power from God to meet that need. The Church of Christ must lay hold of the equipment of the apostolic period for dealing with the ongoing influx of evil spirit hosts among her members. Believers today may receive the equipment of the Holy Spirit whereby the authority of Christ over the demon hosts of Satan is manifested, for this is proved not only by the instance of Philip the deacon in the Acts of the Apostles, but also by the writings of the "Fathers"* in the early

* See Appendix.

centuries of the Christian era. These writings show that the Christians of that time (1) recognized the existence of evil spirits, (2) knew that they influenced, deceived and possessed men, and (3) believed that Christ gave His followers authority over them through His name. And this authority through the name of Christ, wielded by the believer walking in living and vital union with Christ, is available for the servants of God even at this present time. The Spirit of God is making this known in many and diverse ways. God gave a recent object lesson through a Chinese Christian, Pastor Hsi, who acted upon the Word of God in simple faith without the questioning caused by the mental difficulties of Western Christendom. And He has awakened a portion of the Church in the West through the latest Revival in Wales—by an outpouring of the Spirit of God which has not only manifested the power of the Holy Spirit at work in the twentieth century as in the days of Pentecost, but has also unveiled the reality of satanic powers in active opposition to God and His people, spotlighting the need among the Spirit-filled children of God for equipment for dealing with them. Incidentally, too, the Revival in Wales has thrown light upon the Scripture records, showing that the highest points of God's manifested power among men are invariably the occasion for concurrent manifestations of the working of Satan. For it was like that when the Son of God came forth from the wilderness conflict with the prince of darkness and found the hidden demons in many lives aroused to malignant activity, so that from all parts of Palestine crowds of victims came to the Man before whom the possessing spirits trembled in impotent rage.

The awakened part of the Church of today has now no doubt of the real existence of spirit-beings of evil, and that there is an organized monarchy of supernatural powers set up in opposition to Christ and His kingdom who are bent upon the eternal ruin of every member of the human race. And these believers know that God is calling them to seek the fullest equipment obtainable for withstanding and resisting these enemies of Christ and His Church.

In order to understand the methodology of this deceiver-prince of the power of the air, and become acute to discern his program and his tactics in deceiving men, we should search the Scriptures thoroughly to obtain a knowledge both of his character and how his evil underlings are able to possess and use the bodies of men.

Distinctions Between Various Satanic Workings

Distinctions between the various workings of prince Satan and his demonic agents should be definitely noted, so as to understand their devious methods at the present day. For to many, the Adversary is merely a tempter, while they little dream of his power as a deceiver (Rev. 12:9), hinderer (1 Thess. 2:18), murderer (John 8:44), liar (John 8:44), accuser (Rev. 12:10), and a false angel of light; and still less do they imagine the hosts of spirits under his command, constantly besetting their path, bent upon deceiving, hindering, and prompting to sin. A vast host is wholly given up to wickedness (Matt. 12:43–45), delighting to do evil, to slay (Mark 5:2–5), to deceive, to destroy (Mark 9:20)—and has access to men of every grade, prompting them to all kinds of wickedness, being satisfied only when success accompanies their wicked plans to ruin the children of men (Matt. 27:3–5).

Satan's Challenge of Christ in the Wilderness

There is, however, a distinction between Satan, the prince of the demons (Matt. 9:34), and his legion of wicked spirits—a difference in rank which is clearly recognized by Christ and may be noted in many parts of the Gospels (Matt. 25:41). We find Satan in person challenging the Lord in the wilderness temptation, and Christ answering him as a person, word for word, and thought for thought, until he retires, foiled by the keen recognition of his tactics by the Son of God (Luke 4:1–13).

We read of the Lord describing him as the "prince of the world" (John 14:30); recognizing him as ruling over a kingdom (Matt. 12:26); using imperative language to him as a person, saying, "Get thee hence"; while to the Jews He describes his character as "sinning from the beginning," and being a "murderer" and a "liar." He is the "father of lies" who "abode not in the truth" (John 8:44, KJV), having departed from the position which he once held as a great archangel of God. Moreover, he is called "that wicked one" (1 John 3:12, KJV), the "Adversary," and that "old serpent" (Rev. 12:9).

In respect of the devil's method of working, the Lord speaks of him as "sowing tares," which are "sons of the evil one," among the wheat, the sons of God's kingdom (Matt. 13:38–39)—thus revealing the Adversary as possessing the skill of a mastermind, who directs, with executive ability, his work as "prince of the world" throughout the whole inhabited earth, having power to place the men who are called his "sons" wherever he wills.

We read, also, of Satan watching to snatch away the seed of the Word of God from all who hear it—once again indicating his executive power in the world-wide direction of his agents, whom the Lord describes as "fowls of the air" (KJV). In His own interpretation of the parable (Matt. 13:3–4, 13, 19; Mark 4:3–4, 14–15; Luke 8:5, 11–12) Jesus said that by these "fowls" (plural) He meant the "evil one" (Gr. *poneros*, Matt. 13:19), "Satan" (Gr. *Satanas*, Mark 4:15), or the "devil" (Gr. *diabolos*, Luke 8:12). We must remember, however, from the general teaching of other parts of the

Scriptures that the devil is but one person, and does much of his work through the wicked spirits he has at his command. For although Satan is able to transport himself with lightning velocity to any part of his world-wide dominions, he is not omnipresent.

THE LORD'S ATTITUDE TO AND RECOGNITION OF SATAN

The Lord was always prepared to meet again the antagonist whom He had foiled in the wilderness, and who had left Him only "for a season" (Luke 4:13). So when He discerned Satan at work in Peter, He exposed him in one swift sentence, even mentioning his name (Matt. 16:23). Addressing the Jews, He likewise stripped aside the mask of the hidden foe and said, "Ye are of your father, the devil" (John 8:44); with keen-edged words He spoke of him as the one who was lying to them and prompting them to kill Him (John 8:40–41).

And when, in a storm on the lake, He is awakened suddenly, He is at once alert to meet the foe, and stands with calm majesty to rebuke the storm which the prince of the power of the air had roused against Him and the disciples (Mark 4:38–39).

In brief, we find the Lord, right on from the wilderness victory, unveiling the powers of darkness as He went forward in steady mastery over them. Behind what appeared "natural," He sometimes discerned a supernatural power which demanded His rebuke. He rebuked the fever in Peter's wife's mother (Luke 4:39), just as He rebuked the evil spirits in other and more manifest forms, while in other instances He simply healed the sufferer by a word.

Now note the vast difference between the attitude of Satan himself to the Lord and that taken by the lesser spirits of evil. Satan, the prince, tempts Jesus, seeks to hinder Him, prompts the Pharisees to oppose Him, hides behind a disciple to divert Him, and finally takes hold of a disciple to betray Him and sways the multitude to put Him to death; but the spirits of evil bowed down before Jesus, beseeching Him to "let them alone" and not to command them to go into the abyss (Luke 8:31).

The realm of this deceiver-prince is specifically mentioned by the Apostle Paul in his description of him as "prince of the power of the air" (Eph. 2:2), the aerial or "heavenly places" being the special sphere of the activity both of Satan and his hierarchy of powers. Even the derogatory name "Beelzebub," meaning "the god of flies," suggestively speaks of the aerial nature of his powers. The Lord's description of Satan's working through "fowls of the air" (Matt. 13:4, 19) strikingly corresponds to these other statements, together with John's language about the "whole world lying in the evil one" (1 John 5:19)—the atmosphere itself being the sphere of operation of these aerial spirits. And this realm in which the whole human race must move is said to be now "in the evil one."

Evil Spirits in the Gospel Records

The Gospel records refer repeatedly to the workings of evil spirits. They show that wherever the Lord moved, the emissaries of Satan sprang into active manifestation in the bodies and minds of those they indwelt, so that the ministry of Christ and His apostles was directed actively against them. Again and again we read: "He went into their synagogues through all Galilee, preaching and casting out demons" (Mark 1:39); He "cast out many demons, and He suffered not the demons to speak, because they knew Him" (Mark 1:34); "Unclean spirits, whensoever they beheld Him, fell down before Him, and cried, saying, Thou art the Son of God" (Mark 3:11). Then came the sending out of the twelve chosen disciples, and again the spirits of evil are taken into account, for "He gave them authority over the unclean spirits" (Mark 6:7). Later He appointed seventy other messengers; they too, as they went forward in their work, found the demons subject to them through His name (Luke 10:17).

Are we to conclude that Judea, Galilee and Syria were in reality overflowing with people who were insane and epileptic? Is it not evident, rather, that the Son of God dealt with the powers of darkness as the active, primary cause of all sin and suffering of this world, and that the aggressive part of His and His disciples' ministry was directed persistently against them? On the one hand, He dealt with the deceiver of the world and bound the "strong man"; on the other, He taught the truth about God to the people, to destroy the lies which the prince of darkness had placed in their minds about His Father and Himself (2 Cor. 4:4).

We find, too, that the Lord clearly recognized the devil behind the opposition of the Pharisees (John 8:44), and in the "hour and power of darkness" (Luke 22:53) behind His persecutors at Calvary. He said that His mission was to "proclaim release to the captives" (Luke 4:18), and He revealed who the captor was when, on the eve of Calvary, He said, "Now is the judgment of this world: now shall the prince of this world be cast out" (John 12:31).

Christ Always Dealt With the Invisible Enemies

The Lord did not spend time attempting to convince the Pharisees of His claims as the Messiah; nor did He take the opportunity of alluring the Jews by yielding to their desires for an earthly king. Is this not striking? His one mission in this world was manifestly to conquer the satanic prince of the world by death on the cross (Heb. 2:14) and thereby deliver the devil's captives from his control.

He had come to destroy the works of the devil and

his invisible hosts (1 John 3:8).

The commission He gave to the twelve, and to the seventy, was exactly in line with His own. He sent them forth and "gave them authority over unclean spirits, to cast them out, and to heal all manner of disease" (Matt. 10:1); to "first bind the strong man" (Mark 3:27), and then to take his goods; to deal with the invisible hosts of Satan first, and then to "preach the gospel."

From all this we learn that there is one Satan, one devil, one prince of the demons, directing all the opposition to Christ and His people; but myriads of wicked spirits called "demons"—lying spirits, deceiving spirits, foul spirits, unclean spirits—are subjectively at work in men. What is their form, and whence their origin, none can positively say. That they are spirit-beings who are evil is alone beyond all doubt; and all who are undeceived and dispossessed from satanic deception become firm witnesses, from personal experience, to their existence and power. They know that things were done to them by spirits, and that those things were evil. Therefore they recognize that there are spirit-beings who pervert, and know that the symptoms, effects and manifestations of demoniacal possession have active, personal agencies behind them. From experience they know that they often have been hindered by these beings. Therefore, reasoning from personal facts, as well as the testimony of Scripture, they know that these malevolent spirits are tempters, liars, accusers, counterfeiters, cruel enemies, haters, murderers, and wicked beyond all the power of man to know.

The names of these evil spirits describe their characters, for they are called "foul," "lying," "unclean," "evil," and "deceiving" spirits, as they are wholly given up to every manner of wickedness, and deception and lying works.

Additional Characteristics of Evil Spirits

What the characteristics of these wicked spirits are,

and how they are able to dwell in the bodies and minds of human beings, will be seen by a careful examination of the specific cases mentioned in the Gospels; as well as their power to interfere with, mislead, and deceive even servants of God, seen from references to them in other portions of the Word of God.

Evil spirits are generally looked upon as "influences," and not as intelligent beings. But their personality and entity and difference in character as distinct intelligences will be seen in the Lord's direct commands to them (Mark 1:25; 5:8; 3:11–12; 9:25); their power of speech (Mark 3:11); their replies to Him, couched in intelligent language (Matt. 8:29); their sensibilities of fear (Luke 8:31); their definite expression of desire (Matt. 8:31); their need of a dwelling place of rest (Matt. 12:43); their intelligent power of decision (Matt. 12:44); their power of agreement with other spirits; their degrees of wickedness (Matt. 12:45); their power of rage (Matt. 8:28); their strength (Mark 5:4); their ability to possess a human being, either singly (Mark 1:26) or as a throng (Mark 5:9); their use of a human being as their medium for "divining" or foretelling the future (Acts 16:16); and their producing a great miracle worker by their power (Acts 8:9–11).

The Rage and Wickedness of Evil Spirits

When evil spirits act in a rage, they act as a combination of the maddest and most wicked persons in existence, but all their evil is done with fullest intelligence and purpose. They know what they do, they know it is evil, terribly evil, and they will to do it. They do it with rage, and with the full swing of malice, enmity and hatred. They act with fury and bestiality like an enraged bull, as if they had no intelligence. And yet with full intelligence they carry on their work, showing the wickedness of their wickedness. They act from an absolutely depraved nature, with diabolical fury, and with an undeviating perseverance. They act with determination, persistency, and with skillful methods, forcing themselves upon mankind, upon the Church, and still more upon the spiritual man.

Varied Manifestations of Evil Spirits Through Persons

Their manifestations through the persons in whom they obtain footing are varied in character, according to the degree and kind of ground they secure for possession. In one Biblical case, the only manifestation of the evil spirit's presence was dumbness (Matt. 9:32), the spirit possibly locating in the vocal organs; in another, the person held by the spirit was "deaf and dumb" (Mark 9:25), and the symptoms included foaming at the mouth, grinding the teeth—all connected with the head—but the hold of the spirit was of such long standing (v. 21) that he could throw his victim down and convulse the whole body (Mark 9:20–22).

In other cases we find merely an "unclean spirit," as with the man in a synagogue—probably so hidden that none would know the man was thus possessed, until, seeing Christ, the spirit cried out with fear, "Art Thou come to destroy us?" (Mark 1:24); or a "spirit of infirmity" (Luke 13:11) in a woman of whom it might be said that she simply required "healing" of some disease, or that she was always tired and only needed proper nutrition and rest—as some would say in the language of the twentieth century.

Again, we find a very advanced case in the man with the "legion," showing that the evil spirits' possession reached such a climax as to make the person appear insane; for his own personality was so mastered by the malignant spirits in possession as to cause him to lose all sense of decency and self-control in the presence of others (Luke 8:27).

Different Kinds of Evil Spirits

That there are different kinds of spirits is evident not only from their manifestations recorded in the Gospels but also in later instances: in the account of the girl at Philippi, possessed by a "spirit of divination"; and in Simon the Sorcerer, who was so energized by satanic power for the working of miracles that he was considered to be "the great power of God" by the deceived people (Acts 8:10, KJV). In these cases, trickery was the game.

Spiritists of today are also deceived if they really believe they are communicating with the spirits of the dead. Surely it is easy for designing spirits to impersonate dead people, including even saintly Christians: they have watched them (Acts 19:15) all their lives, and can easily imitate their personality traits and counterfeit their voices.

Evil Spirits Foretelling Through Mediums

In like manner as a "spirit of divination," evil spirits can use "palmists" and "fortune tellers" to deceive; they can inspire mediums to foretell events. Not that they actually know the future—for God alone has this knowledge—but the spirits observe human beings and know also what they themselves intend to do. So if they can get the person to whom these things are told to cooperate with them, by accepting or believing their "foretelling," they will attempt to bring these things about. That is, the medium says such and such a thing will happen, the person believes it, and by believing opens himself, or herself, to the evil spirit, to bring that thing to pass. Of course, the spirits cannot always succeed—and this is the reason why there is so much uncertainty about such prognostications—because many things may hinder the workings of the evil spirit-beings, particularly the prayers of friends or intercessors in the Christian Church.

These are some of the "deep things of Satan" (Rev.

2:24) mentioned by the Lord in His message to Thyatira, manifestly referring to far more subtle workings among the Christians of that time than all that the apostles had seen in the cases recorded in the Gospels. "The mystery of lawlessness doth already work," wrote the Apostle Paul (2 Thess. 2:7). So deep-laid schemes of deception and distortion through devil-inspired doctrines (1 Tim. 4:1)—foretold as reaching their full culmination in the last days—were already at work in the Church of God. Yes, evil spirits are at work today, inside as well as outside the professing Church. For "spiritualism," in its meaning of having dealings with spirits, may be found inside Christendom, even among the most earnest people. Men think that because they have never been to a seance they are free from spiritism, not knowing that evil spirits attack and deceive every human being. They do not confine their working to the professing Church, or the world, but operate wherever they can find conditions fulfilled to enable them to manifest their power.

The Power of Evil Spirits Over Human Bodies

The control of spirits over the bodies of those they possess is seen in several Gospel cases. The man with the legion was not master over his own body or mind. The spirits would "seize him," "drive him" (Luke 8:29), compel him to cut himself with stones (Mark 5:5), strengthen him to burst every fetter and chain (v. 4), "cry out" aloud (v. 5), and fiercely attack others (Matt. 8:28). The boy with the dumb spirit would be dashed to the ground (Luke 9:42), and convulsed; the spirit forced him to cry out, and tore him, so that his body became bruised and sore (v. 39). Teeth, tongue, vocal organs, ears, eyes, nerves and muscles are seen to be affected and interfered with by evil spirits in possession. Weakness and strength are both produced by their working, and men (Mark 1:23), women (Luke 8:2), boys (Mark 9:17), and girls (Mark 7:25) are equally open to their power.

That the Jews were familiar with the fact of evil-spirit possession is clear from their words when they saw the Lord Christ cast out the blind and dumb spirit from a man (Matt. 12:24). It is evident also that there were men among them who knew some method of dealing with such cases (v. 27). "By whom do your sons cast them out?" asked the Lord. That such dealing with evil spirits was not truly effective may be gathered from the several instances given, where it appears that alleviation of the sufferings from evil-spirit possession was the most that could be done: *e.g.* (1) the case of King Saul, who was soothed by the harp playing of David; (2) the sons of Sceva, who were professional exorcists, yet who recognized a power in the name of Jesus which their exorcism did not possess. In both these cases, the danger connected with the attempted alleviation or exorcism, because of the power of the evil spirits to resist, is strikingly shown in contrast to the complete results achieved by Christ and His apostles. David playing to Saul is suddenly aware of the javelin flung by the hand of the man he was seeking to soothe. And the sons of Sceva found the possessed man leaping upon them, and overpowering them, when they used the name of Jesus without the divine co-working given to all who exercise personal faith in Him.

Among the heathen also—who know the venom of similar wicked spirits—the best that can be accomplished is mere propitiation and the soothing of the spirits' hatred, by obedience to them.

The Exorcism of Evil Spirits Contrasted With Christ's Power of Word

How striking it is to contrast all this with the calm authority of Christ. He needed no rubric of adjuration, nor other formula of exorcism, and no prolonged preparation of Himself before dealing with a spirit-possessed individual. "He cast out the spirits by a word." "With authority and power He commandeth . . . and they obey Him," was the wondering testimony of the awe-struck people. It was the testimony, also, of the seventy sent forth by Him to use the authority of His name. They found that the spirits were subject to them, even as they were to the Lord (Luke 10:17–20).

"They obey Him," said the people. "They"—the evil spirits whom the people knew to be real identities, governed by Beelzebub, their prince (Matt. 12:24–27). The complete mastery of Jesus over the demons compelled the religious leaders to find some way of explaining His authority over them. And so by that subtle influence of Satan with which all who have had insight into his devices are familiar, they cunningly accuse the Lord of having satanic power Himself, saying, "He casteth out demons through Beelzebub, the prince of the demons."

This reference to Satan and his position as a prince was left uncontradicted by the Lord. In the face of Satan's lie, Jesus simply declared the truth that He cast out demons "by the finger of God," and the fact that Satan's kingdom would soon fall were he to act against himself and dislodge his emissaries from their place of retreat in human bodies. That Satan does apparently fight against himself is sometimes true; but when he does so, it is only for the purpose of covering up some scheme—for greater advantage to his kingdom.

The Authority Over Evil Spirits by the Apostles After Pentecost

That the apostles after Pentecost recognized and dealt with the denizens of the invisible world is evident both from the Acts of the Apostles and from references in the Epistles. During their three years' training by the Lord, the disciples were being prepared for Pentecost and the exposure to the supernatural world resulting from the coming of the Holy Spirit. They had watched Jesus deal with the wicked spirits of Satan, and had themselves learned to deal with them too. So the power of the Holy Spirit could be safely given at Pentecost to men who already knew the workings of the foe. We see how quickly Peter recognized Satan's work in Ananias (Acts 5:3), and how unclean spirits came out at his presence even as they had with his Lord (Acts 5:16). Philip likewise found the evil hosts subservient to the word of his testimony (Acts 8:7) as he proclaimed Christ to the people. And Paul definitely knew the power of the name of the risen Lord (Acts 19:11) in dealing with the powers of evil.

It is therefore clear from Bible history that the manifestation of the power of God invariably meant active dealing with the satanic hosts; that the manifestation of the power of God at Pentecost, and through the apostles' subsequent ministry, meant an aggressive attitude toward the powers of darkness. We can therefore conclude that growth and maturation of the Church at the end of the New Testament dispensation will require the same recognition and the same attitude toward these satanic hosts—with the same co-witness of the Holy Spirit to the authority of the name of Jesus—as was found in the early Church. In brief, the Church of Christ will reach its high-water mark when it is able to recognize and deal with demon possession: when it knows how to "bind the strong man" by prayer and "command" the spirits of evil in the name of Christ, thus delivering men and women from their power.

The Church in the Twentieth Century Must Recognize the Powers of Darkness

To this end the Christian Church must recognize that the existence of deceiving, lying spirits is as real in the twentieth century as in the time of Christ and that their attitude toward the human race is unchanged:

that their one ceaseless aim is to deceive every human being. Yes, that they are given up to wickedness all day long, and all night long, and that they are ceaselessly and actively pouring a stream of wickedness into the world and are satisfied only when they succeed in their wicked plans to deceive and ruin men.

Yet the servants of God have been concerned only to destroy their *works*—to deal with *sin*—not recognizing the need of using the power given by Christ to resist by faith and prayer this ever-flowing flood of satanic power pouring in among men. Hence both men and women, young and old, Christian and non-Christian, become deceived through their guile, because of ignorance about them and their wiles.

These supernatural forces of Satan are the true hindrance to revival. The power of God which in 1904 broke forth in Wales, with all the marks of the days of Pentecost, was checked and hindered from going on to its fullest purpose by the same influx of evil spirits as met the Lord Christ on earth and the apostles of the early Church—with the difference that this inroad of the powers of darkness found the Christians of the twentieth century, with few exceptions, unable to recognize and deal with them. Evil-spirit possession has followed and checked every similar revival throughout the centuries since Pentecost. If the Church is to advance to maturity, these things must now be understood and dealt with—understood not only with respect to the degrees of possession recorded in the Gospels and Acts, but in light of the special forms of manifestation suited to the close of the age. For now these spirits have appeared *under the guise of the Holy Spirit,* yet having some of the very characteristic marks in bodily symptoms which are seen in the Gospel accounts, when all who observed the manifestations knew that it was the work of the spirits of Satan.

CHAPTER 3

Deception by Evil Spirits in Modern Times

In the extraordinary onslaught of the deceiver which will come upon the whole of Christendom at the close of the age, through his army of deceiving spirits, there are some, more than others, who will for a particular reason be attacked by the powers of darkness. These individuals need clear light as to his deceptive workings, so that they may pass through the trial of the "last hour" and be counted worthy to escape that hour of *greater* trial which is coming upon the earth (Luke 21:34–36; Rev. 3:10).

These are the ones who are recklessly ready to follow the Lord at any cost, and yet do not realize their unpreparedness for contest with the spiritual powers of the unseen world as they press on into fuller spiritual things. They are believers who are full of mental conceptions wrought into them in earlier years—views and opinions which hinder the Spirit of God from preparing them for all they will meet as they press on to their coveted goal, and which also hinder others from giving them from the Scriptures much that they need to know regarding the spiritual world into which they are so blindly advancing. These sentiments lull them into a false security, and give ground for, and even help bring about, that very deception which enables the deceiver to find them an easy prey.

CAN "HONEST SOULS" BE DECEIVED?

One prevailing idea which such believers have deeply embedded in their minds is that "honest seekers after God" will not be allowed to be deceived. This is one of Satan's lies to lure such seekers into a false position of safety. It is proved by the history of the Church during the past two thousand years, for every "wile of error" which has borne sad fruit throughout this period laid hold first of devoted believers who were "honest souls." The errors among groups of such believers, some well known to the present generation, all began among "honest" people—and all so sure that, knowing the sidetracking of others before them, they would never be caught by the wiles of Satan. Yet they, too, have been deceived by lying spirits counterfeiting the workings of God.

Among such, lying spirits have sometimes worked on their determination *literally* to obey the Scriptures, and by misuse of the letter of the written Word have pushed them into awkward corners of unbalanced truth, with resulting erroneous practices. Many who have suffered for their strict adherence to these "Biblical commands" firmly believe that they are martyrs suffering for Christ.

The aftermath of the Revival in Wales, which was a true work of God, revealed many swept off their feet by evil supernatural effects, which they were not able to distinguish from the true working of God. And since that time there have been "movements" in other places, with large numbers of followers, swept into deception through the wiles of deceiving spirits counterfeiting the workings of God. All are "honest souls," deceived by the subtle foe, and certain to be led on into still deeper deception, notwithstanding their honesty and earnestness, unless they are awakened to "return to soberness" and recovery out of the snare of the devil into which they have fallen (2 Tim. 2:26).

FAITHFULNESS TO LIGHT NOT SUFFICIENT SAFEGUARD AGAINST DECEPTION

We need to know that to be true in motive, and faithful up to light, is not sufficient safeguard against deception; and that it is not safe to rely upon "honesty of purpose" as guaranteeing protection from the enemy's wiles, instead of taking heed to the warnings of God's Word and watching unto prayer.

Christians who are true and faithful and honest can be deceived by Satan and his deceiving spirits, for the following reasons:

(1) When a man becomes a child of God by the regenerating power of the Spirit—giving him new life as he trusts in the atoning work of Christ—he does not at the same time receive fullness of knowledge, either about God, himself, or the devil.

(2) The mind, which by nature is darkened (Eph. 4:18) and under a veil created by Satan (2 Cor. 4:4), is only renewed, and the veil destroyed, *up to the extent that the light of truth penetrates it,* and according to the measure in which the man is able to apprehend it.

(3) "Deception" has to do with the *mind,* and by definition is the result of a thought being admitted to the mind under the erroneous assumption that it is truth. Since deception is based on ignorance, and not on one's moral character, a Christian who is "true and faithful" up to the knowledge he has is yet open to deception in the spheres where he is ignorant. We are liable to be deceived by the devil because of *ignorance* (2 Cor. 2:11).

(4) The thought that God will protect a believer from being deceived if he is true and faithful is in itself a deception, because it throws a man off guard, and ignores the fact that there are *conditions* on the part of the believer which have to be fulfilled for God's working. God does not do anything *instead* of a man, but by the man's *cooperation* with Him; *neither does He un-*

dertake to make up for a man's ignorance, when He has already provided knowledge for him which will prevent him from being deceived.

(5) Christ would not have warned His disciples, "Take heed . . . be not deceived," if there had been *no danger of deception,* or if God had undertaken to keep them from deception apart from their "taking heed" and their knowledge of such danger.

We must not lower our spiritual guard. The knowledge that it is *possible* to be deceived keeps the mind open to truth and light from God, and is one of the primary conditions for the keeping power of God; whereas a mind closed to light and truth is a certain guarantee of deception by Satan at his earliest opportunity.

As we glance back over the history of the Church, and study the rise of various "heresies" or "aberrant belief systems"—as they have sometimes been called—we can at times detect that the period of deception began with some great crisis, a crisis in which a particular individual was motivated to give himself up in full abandonment to the Holy Spirit, and in so doing he opened himself to the supernatural powers of the invisible world.

The reason for the peril of such a crisis is that, up to this time, that believer used his reasoning faculties in judging right and wrong, and obeyed what he believed to be the will of God from *principle;* but now, in his abandonment to the Holy Spirit, he begins to obey an unseen Person, and to submit his faculties and his reasoning powers in blind obedience to that which he believes is of God. The will is surrendered to carry out the will of God at all costs, and the whole being is made subject to the powers of the unseen world. The believer, of course, purposes that it shall only be to the power of God, not taking into account that there are other powers in the metaphysical realm, and that all that is "supernatural" is not entirely of God. Not realizing that, this absolute surrender of his whole being to invisible forces *without knowing how to discern between the contrary powers of God and Satan* is the gravest risk to the inexperienced believer.

The question whether this surrender to "*obey the Spirit*" is one that is in accord with Scripture should be examined in view of the way in which so many wholehearted believers have been misled, for it is strange that an attitude which is scriptural should be so grievously the cause of danger, and often of complete wreckage.

Is the Expression "Obey the Spirit" Scriptural?

"The Holy Ghost, whom God hath given to them that obey Him," is the principal phrase giving rise to the expression "obey the Spirit." It was used by Peter before the priestly council in Jerusalem, but nowhere else in the Scriptures is the same thought given. The whole passage needs to be read carefully to reach a clear conclusion. "We must obey God" (Acts 5:29), Peter declared to the Sanhedrin, for "we are witnesses . . . and so is the Holy Ghost whom God hath given to them *that obey Him*" (v. 32). Does the apostle mean "obey the *Spirit*" or "obey *God*," according to the first words of the passage? The distinction is important, and the sense of the words can be rightly grasped only by noting the teaching of other parts of Scripture, that the Triune God in heaven is to be obeyed through the power of the indwelling Spirit of God. For to place the Holy Ghost as the *object* of obedience, rather than God the Father, through the Son, by the Holy Spirit, creates the danger of leading the believer to rely upon, or obey, a "spirit" in or around him, rather than God on the throne in heaven. God is to be obeyed by the child of God united to His Son—*the Holy Spirit being the medium, or means, through whom God* is worshiped and obeyed.

THE TRUE WORK OF THE HOLY SPIRIT IN THE BELIEVER

The Holy Spirit should never become the center and object of thought and worship, a place which He Himself does not desire, and which it is not the purpose of the Father in heaven that He should have or occupy. "He shall not speak from Himself" (John 16:13), said the Lord Jesus before Calvary, as He foretold the Spirit's coming at Pentecost. He would act as Teacher (John 14:26), but teaching the words of Another, not His own; He would bear witness to Another, not to Himself (John 15:26); He would glorify Another, not Himself (John 16:14); He would only speak what was given Him to speak by Another (John 16:13). In brief, the Spirit's entire work would be to lead souls into union with the Son and give proper knowledge of the Father in heaven, while *He Himself directed and worked in the background.*

If a man who is untaught in the scriptural statements about the work of the Triune God makes "obeying the Spirit" his supreme purpose, the deceiver will aim to counterfeit the guidance of the Spirit, and even the presence of the Spirit Himself.

It is just here that the ignorance of the seeker about (1) the spiritual world now opened to him, (2) the working of evil powers in that realm, and (3) the conditions upon which God works in and through him, gives the enemy his opportunity. It becomes the time of greatest peril for anyone unless he is instructed and prepared by the Lord, as the disciples were for three whole years. The danger lies in the area of supernatural "guidance," for one must know the conditions of cooperation with the Holy Spirit in order to discern the will of God and and be able to recognize counterfeit manifestations. The "discerning of spirits" is required to detect the workings of the false angel of light, for he is able to bring about counterfeit gifts of prophecy, tongues, healings, and other spiritual experiences connected with the work of the Holy Ghost.

Those who have their eyes opened to the opposing forces of the metaphysical realm understand that very few believers can guarantee that they are obeying *God and God only, in directly supernatural guidance,* because there are so many factors liable to intervene, such as the believer's own mind, spirit, or will, and the deceptive intrusion of the powers of darkness.

Knowledge is essential here. Scripture teaches that there is a God-given gift of "discerning of spirits" (1 Cor. 12:10) which enables one to detect that an unwelcome spirit is at work, but there is also a test of spirits which is doctrinal (1 John 4:1–6). In the former, a believer can discern in his spirit that lying spirits are at work in a meeting, or in a person, but he may not have the understanding needed for testing the *doctrines* being set forth by the teacher. He needs a level of knowledge in both cases: knowledge to read his spirit with assurance in the face of all contrary appearances, that the supernatural workings are not "of God," and knowledge to detect the subtlety of "teachings" bearing certain infallible indications that they emanate from the pit, even while appearing to be from God.

As to *personal* obedience to God, the believer can detect whether or not he is obeying *God* in some "command" by judging its fruits, and by being aware of the character of God—such as the truth that (1) God has always a purpose in His commands, and (2) He will give no command out of harmony with His character and Word. (Other factors needed for clear knowledge we will deal with later on.)

The Need for Examination of Theories

Is it not becoming clear, in light of the existence of deceiving spirits and their methods of deception, that close examination is needed of modern theories, conceptions, and expressions concerning things in connection with God and His way of working in man? For only the truth of God, apart from "views" of truth, will avail for protection or for successful warfare in the conflict with wicked spirits in the heavenly sphere.

All that is in any degree the outcome of the mind of the "natural man" (1 Cor. 2:14) will prove to be but weapons of straw in this great battle, and if we rely upon others' "views of truth," or upon our own *human conceptions* of truth, Satan will use these very things to deceive us—even building us up in these theories and views so that under cover of them he may accomplish his purposes.

We cannot, therefore, at this time, overestimate the importance of believers having ready minds to "examine all things" they have thought, and perhaps taught, in connection with the things of God and the spiritual realm—all the "truths" they have held, all the phrases and expressions they have used in "holiness teachings," and all the ideas they have absorbed through others. For any wrong *interpretation* of truth, any theories and phrases which are man-conceived and which we may build upon wrongly, will have perilous consequences to ourselves and others in the conflict which the Church and the individual believer is now passing through. Since in the "later times" evil spirits will come to them with deceptions in DOCTRINAL form, believers must examine carefully what they accept as "doctrine," lest it should be from the emissaries of the deceiver.

THE SPIRITUAL BELIEVER EXHORTED TO "JUDGE ALL THINGS"

The duty of this examination of spiritual things is strongly urged by the Apostle Paul, again and again. "He that is spiritual *judgeth* [margin, *examineth*, or, as in the Greek, *investigates and decides*] all things" (1 Cor. 2:15). The "spiritual" believer is to use his renewed judgment, and this spiritual examination is mentioned as operative in connection with "things of the Spirit of God" (1 Cor. 2:14). God Himself respects the intelligence of the man He re-creates in Christ, and invites that man to judge and examine His own workings by His Spirit. So even "the things of the Spirit" are not to be received as truly of Him without being examined and "spiritually discerned" as of God. When, therefore, it is maintained in connection with the supernatural and abnormal manifestations of the present time that it is not necessary, and not according to the will of God, for believers to understand or explain all the workings of God, it is out of accord with the apostle's statement that "he that is spiritual *judgeth all things*" and consequently should *reject* all things which his spiritual judgment is unable to accept, until such a time as he is able to discern with clearness what are the things of God.

And not only is the believer to discern or judge the things of the spirit—*i.e.*, all things in the spiritual realm—but he is also to judge himself. For "if we discriminated ourselves"—the Greek word means *to make a thorough investigation*—we would not need the dealing of the Lord to bring to light the things in ourselves which we have failed to discern by discrimination (1 Cor. 11:31, mg.).

"Brethren, be not children in mind: howbeit in malice be ye babes, but in mind BE MEN" (Gr., of *full* or *mature* age, 1 Cor. 14:20) wrote the apostle again to the Corinthians, as he explained to them the way of the working of the Spirit among them. The believer is in "mind" to be of "full age"; that is, able to examine, "bring to the proof" (2 Tim. 4:2, mg.), and "*prove all things*" (1 Thess. 5:21). He is to abound in knowledge and "all discernment," so as to "distinguish the things that differ," that he may be "sincere and void of offence unto the day of Christ" (Phil. 1:9–10, mg.).

EXPRESSIONS, "VIEWS," DOCTRINES, NEED TO BE EXAMINED

In accordance with these directions of the Word of God, and in view of the critical time through which the Church is passing, every expression, "view," or theory which we hold concerning things should now be examined carefully, and brought to the proof, with open and honest desire to know the pure truth of God—as well as every statement that comes to our knowledge from the experience of others, which may throw light upon our own pathway. Every criticism—just or unjust—should be humbly received and *examined to discover its ground,* apparent or real; and facts concerning spiritual verities from every section of the Church of God should be analyzed, independent of their pleasure or pain to us personally—either for our own enlightenment or for our equipment in the service of God. For the knowledge of truth is the first essential for warfare with the lying spirits of Satan, and truth must be eagerly sought for and faced with earnest and sincere desire to know it and obey it in the light of God: truth concerning ourselves, discerned by unbiased discrimination; truth from the Scriptures, uncolored, unstrained, unmutilated, undiluted; truth in facing facts of experience in all members of the Body of Christ, and not in one section alone.

THE PLACE OF TRUTH IN DELIVERANCE

There is a fundamental principle involved in the freeing power of truth from the deceptions of the devil. DELIVERANCE FROM BELIEVING LIES MUST BE BY BELIEVING TRUTH. Nothing can remove a lie but truth. "Ye shall know the truth, and the truth shall make you free" (John 8:32) is applicable to every aspect of truth, as well as the special truth referred to by the Lord when He spoke those pregnant words.

In the very first stage of the Christian life, the sinner

must know the truth of the gospel if he is to be saved. Christ is the Saviour, but He saves through, and not apart from, instruments or means. If the believer needs freedom, he must seek the Son of God for it too. And how does the Son set free? *By the Holy Spirit*, and the Holy Spirit does it by the instrumentality of truth. So we may say, in brief, freedom is the gift of the Son, by the Holy Spirit working through *truth*.

There are three stages in apprehending truth:

(1) Perception of truth by the understanding.
(2) Perception of truth for use, and personal application.
(3) Perception of truth for teaching, and passing on to others.

Truth apparently not grasped may lie passive in the mind, and then in the hour of one's need suddenly emerge into experience, and thus by experience become clear to the mind in which it has been lying dormant. It is only by continual application and assimilation of truth into experience, however, that it becomes sufficiently clarified in one's mind that it may be taught to others.

All believers greatly need to eagerly seek *truth* for their progressive liberation from Satan's many lies; for knowledge of truth alone can give victory over the deceiver. If, however, a hearer of truth should resist it, or rebel against it, that unattended-to truth can well be left to the care of the Holy Spirit of Truth. Even in the case of resistance to truth it has at least reached the *mind*, and at any time may fructify into experience.

There are three attitudes of mind with regard any item of knowledge:

(1) Assuming you know the matter already.
(2) Being neutral toward it; admitting "I do not know."
(3) Being certain of its accuracy.

This is instanced in the life of Christ. Some said of Him, "He is a false prophet," with an *assumption* of knowledge; others said, "We do not know"—taking a position of neutrality until they did know; but Peter said, "We *know* . . ."—and he had true knowledge.

The Safety of a Neutral Attitude to All Supernatural Manifestations

When believers first hear of the possibility of counterfeits of God and divine things, they almost invariably ask, "How are we to know which is which?" It is enough, first of all, for them to know that such counterfeits are possible. Then, as they mature and seek light from God, they shall learn to know for themselves, in a way that no human being can explain to them.

But they cry, "We do not know, and how can we know?" Well, they should remain neutral to all supernatural workings until they do know. There is among many seekers a wrong anxiety to know, as if that knowledge alone would extricate them. They think that they must be solidly for or against certain things, things which they cannot decide are from God or an occult source. They desire to know infallibly which is which, that they may declare their position. But believers should take only a tentative attitude of "for" or "against" while uncertain whether the things in doubt are divine or satanic—maintaining the wisdom and safety of the neutral position. In time, by a means which cannot be fully described, they will know what they have wanted to understand.

Over-eagerness in desiring certitude can result in mental suffering, restless anxiety, worry and grief, which can cause a loss of moral poise and power. It is important in seeking one "blessing" not to destroy another. In seeking certainty in these spiritual matters let not the believer lose patience, and calm, quiet restfulness and faith. Let him watch himself, lest the enemy gain advantage, and rob him of moral power even while he is keen to get light regarding the way of victory.

A Mistaken Conception About the Shelter of the Blood

Before we move on, some misinterpretations of truth which are giving ground to the powers of darkness at this time, and which need examination to discover how far they are in accord with Scripture, should be briefly looked into.

First: *a mistaken conception about the "shelter of the blood," claimed upon an assembly as a guarantee of absolute protection from the working of the powers of darkness.*

The New Testament "proportion of truth" concerning the application of Jesus' blood by the Holy Spirit may be summarized as follows: (1) The blood of Jesus *cleanses from sin* (*a*) "if we walk in the light," and (*b*) "if we confess our sins" (1 John 1:7, 9). (2) The blood of Jesus *gives access to the Holiest of all*, because of the cleansing power from sin (Hebrews 10:19). (3) The blood of Jesus *is the ground of victory* over Satan, because of its cleansing from every confessed sin, and because at Calvary Satan was conquered (Rev. 12:11). But nowhere do we read that any person can be put "under the blood" apart from his own volition and individual condition before God. Therefore, if the "shelter of the blood" is claimed over an assembly of people and someone present is giving ground to Satan, the "claiming of the blood" does not avail to prevent Satan from working on the ground to which he has a right in that person.

This misconception about the protecting power of the blood is serious; for those who are present at a meeting where Satan as well as God is working may believe they are personally safe from Satan's workings apart from their individual condition and dealing with

God. But through the ground they have given—even unknowingly—to the Adversary, they are open to his power.

Mistaken Conceptions Concerning "Waiting for the Spirit"

Second: *mistaken conceptions concerning "waiting for the Spirit" to descend.*

Here again we find expressions and theories misleading, and opening the door to satanic deceptions. "If we want a Pentecostal manifestation of the Spirit, we must 'tarry,' as did the disciples before Pentecost," some of us have proclaimed; and we have seized upon the text in Luke 24:49 and Acts 1:4, and passed the word along, "Yes, we must 'tarry'"—until, compelled by the inroads of the Adversary in "waiting meetings" we have had to search the Scriptures once more, to discover that the Old Testament word of "wait on the Lord," so often used in the Psalms, has been strained beyond the New Testament proportion of truth and exaggerated into a "waiting on God" for the outpouring of the Spirit . . . which has even gone beyond the ten days which preceded Pentecost, into four months, and even four years, and which, to our knowledge, has ended in an influx of deceiving spirits which has rudely awakened some of the waiting souls.

The actual scriptural truth concerning "waiting for the Spirit" may be summed up as follows:

(1) The disciples waited ten days, but we have no indication that they "waited" in any passive state, but rather in simple prayer and supplication—until the fullness of time had come for the fulfillment of the promise of the Father.

(2) The command to wait given by the Lord (Acts 1:4) was not carried forward into the Christian dispensation after the Holy Ghost had come—for in no single instance, either in the Acts or in the Epistles, do the apostles bid the disciples to "tarry" for the gift of the

Holy Spirit. Rather, they use the word "receive" in every instance (Acts 19:2).*

It is true that at this present time Christendom is, as a whole, living experientially on the wrong side of Pentecost; but in our dealing with God individually for the reception of the Holy Spirit, this does not put the seekers back to the position of the disciples before the Holy Ghost had been given by the Ascended Lord. The Risen Lord poured forth the stream of the Spirit again and again after the Day of Pentecost, but in each instance it was without "tarrying" as the disciples did at the first (see Acts 4:31). The Holy Spirit, who proceeds from the Father through the Son to His people, is now among them, waiting to give Himself unceasingly to all who will appropriate and receive Him (John 15:26; Acts 2:33, 38–39). A "waiting for the Spirit," therefore, is not in accord with the general tenor of truth given in the Acts and the Epistles. Scripture shows, rather, the imperative call to the believer to put in his claim, not only to his identification with the Lord Jesus in His death and to union in life with Him in His resurrection, but also to the enduement for witnessing which came to the disciples on the Day of Pentecost.

On the believer's side, we may say, however, that there is a waiting while the Holy Spirit deals with and prepares the one who has put in his claim, until he is in the right attitude for the influx of the Holy Spirit into his spirit—but this is substantially different from the "waiting for Him to come" which has opened the door so frequently to satanic manifestations from the unseen world. The Lord does take the believer at his word when he puts in his claim for his share of the Pentecostal gift, but the "manifestation of the Spirit"—the evidence of His indwelling and outworking—may not be

---

* The Greek word used for receiving the Holy Spirit carries the force of "grasping"—just the opposite condition to passivity.

according to any preconceptions of the seeker.

Why Waiting Meetings Are Profitable to Evil Spirits

Why "waiting meetings"—that is, "waiting for the Spirit" until He descends in some manifested way—have been so profitable to deceiving spirits is because they are not in accord with the written Word, where it is set forth that (1) The Holy Spirit is not to be prayed to, or asked to come, as He is the Gift of Another (see Luke 11:13; John 14:16). (2) The Holy Spirit is not to be "waited for," but to be taken, or RECEIVED from the hand of the Risen Lord (John 20:22; Eph. 5:18); of whom it is written, "He shall baptize you with the Holy Ghost and with fire" (Matt. 3:11). Because out of line with the truth of the Scriptures, therefore "prayer to the Spirit," "trust in the Spirit," "obeying the Spirit," "expecting the Spirit to descend," may all become prayer, trust, and obedience to evil spirits when they counterfeit the working of God.

Other mistaken conceptions of spiritual truth center around phrases such as these: *"God can do everything. If I trust Him He must keep me"*—not understanding that God works according to laws and conditions, and that those who trust Him should seek to know the conditions upon which He can work in response to their trust. *"If I were wrong, God would not use me"*—not understanding that if a man is right in his will, God will use him to the fullest extent possible, but this being "used" of God is no guarantee that any man is *absolutely right in all that he says and does.*

Another is *"I have no sin,"* or *"Sin has been entirely removed"*—not knowing how deeply the sinful life of Adam is ingrained in the fallen creation, and how the assumption that "sin" has been eliminated from the whole being enables the enemy to keep the life of nature from being dealt with by the continual power of the cross.

"God, who is Love, will not allow me to be deceived" is of itself a deception, based on ignorance of the depths of the Fall, and the misconception that God works irrespective of spiritual laws. *"I do not believe it possible for a Christian to be deceived"* is a shutting of the eyes to facts around us on every hand. *"I have had too long an experience to need teaching"*; or *"I must be taught of God directly, because it is written, 'Ye need not that any man teach you'"* is the misuse of another passage of Scripture, which some believers interpret as meaning that they are to refuse all spiritual teaching through others. But that the apostle's words "Ye need not that any man teach you" did not preclude God from teaching through anointed teachers is shown by the inclusion of "teachers" in the list of gifted believers to the Church, for "the building up of the Body of Christ . . . through that which every joint supplieth" (Eph. 4:11–16). For God is sometimes able to teach His children more quickly by indirect means—that is, through others—than directly, because men are so slow in understanding the way of direct teaching by the Spirit of God.

Many other similar misconceptions of spiritual things by Christians of today give opportunity to deception by the enemy, because they cause believers to close their minds to (1) the statements of God's Word; (2) the facts of life; and (3) the help of others who could throw light upon the way (1 Peter 1:12).

The Dangers of Coined Phrases to Express Spiritual Truths

Other dangers center around the coining of phrases to describe some special experience. This includes words in familiar use among earnest children of God who attend conventions: such as "possess," "control," "surrender," "let go"—all containing truth in relation to God, but because of the *interpretation* of them in the minds of many believers, liable to bring about conditions for the evil spirits of Satan to "possess" and "control" those who "surrender" and "let go" to the powers of the spiritual world—if they know not how to discern between the working of God and Satan.

Various preconceptions of the way God works also give evil spirits their opportunity: such as, that when a believer is supernaturally *compelled* to act, it is a special evidence that *God* is guiding him; or that if God brings all things to our "remembrance" we need not use our memories at all.

Other thoughts which are liable to bring about the passive conditions which evil spirits need for their deceptive workings may also be through the following misconceptions of truth:

(1) "Christ lives in me," *i.e., I* do not live now at all.
(2) "Christ lives in me," *i.e.*, I have lost my personality, because Christ is now personally in me, based on Galatians 2:20.
(3) "God works in me," *i.e.*, I need not work, only surrender and obey, based on Philippians 2:13.
(4) "God wills instead of me," *i.e.*, I must not use my will at all.
(5) "God is the only one to judge," *i.e.*, I must not use my judgment.
(6) "I have the mind of Christ," so I must not have any mind of my own, based on 1 Corinthians 2:16.
(7) "God speaks to me," so I must not "think" or "reason," only "obey" what He tells me to do.
(8) "I wait on God," and "I must not act until He moves me."
(9) "God reveals His will to me by visions," so I do not need to decide, and use my reason and conscience.
(10) "I am crucified with Christ," therefore "I am *dead*," and must "practice" death, which I conceive to be passivity of feeling, thinking, etc.

To carry out in practice these various conceptions of truth, the believer quenches all personal action of mind, judgment, reason, will and activity in order for the "divine life to flow" through him, whereas God needs the fullest liberation of the faculties of the man, and his active and intelligent cooperation in will, for the working out of all these spiritual truths in experience.

The following table will show some other misinterpretations of truth which need clarifying in the minds of many children of God:

TRUTH	TRUE INTERPRETATION	INCORRECT INTERPRETATION
1. "The blood of Jesus cleanseth . . ."	Cleanses moment by moment.	Leaves the man sinless.
2. "It is not ye that speak . . ."	The source is not from the believer.	* The man must not speak nor use his jaws, but be passive.
3. "Ask and ye shall receive."	Ask according to *God's will* and you will receive.	† Ask *anything*, and you will receive.
4. "It is God that worketh in you to will and to do . . ."	The man must "will" and must act.	* God wills for you (or *instead* of you) and God works *instead* of you.
5. "Ye need not that any man teach you."	You do not need any *man* to teach you, but you need Spirit-taught teachers given of God.	‡ I must not take teaching from any man, but "direct" from God . . .

* These two wrongly interpreted passages offer a basis for passivity.

† Leads to haphazard and unintelligent praying, without seeking to know the will of God.

‡ By this attitude, the "adding to faith" of knowledge is greatly hindered, and those who assume this attitude take an evil, infallible position, and their advancement in the spiritual life is impeded.

TRUTH	TRUE INTERPRETATION	INCORRECT INTERPRETATION
6. "He will guide you into all truth . . ."	The Spirit of God will guide, but I must see *how* and when . . .	‡ He *has* guided me into all truth . . .
7. "A people for His own possession . . ."	God's ownership.	"Possessed" by God indwelling, moving and controlling a passive automaton.
8. "Meet for the Master's use . . ."	God, in the man's spirit, using the mind, in the sense of giving light for the believer's intelligent cooperation.	"Used" by God as a passive tool, requiring blind submission.

‡ By this attitude, the "adding to faith" of knowledge is greatly hindered, and those who assume this attitude take an evil, infallible position, and their advancement in the spiritual life is impeded.

What, then, is the condition for safety from the deception of evil spirits? (1) Knowledge that they exist; (2) recognition that they can deceive the most honest believers (Gal. 2:11–16); (3) an understanding of the conditions and ground necessary for their working, so as to give them no place, and no opportunity of working; and, lastly, (4) intelligent knowledge of God, and how to cooperate with Him in the power of the Holy Spirit. To make these points clear will be our purpose in succeeding pages.

CHAPTER 4

The Perils of Passivity

The chief condition for the working of evil spirits in a human being, apart from sin, is passivity, the exact opposite to the condition which God requires for His working. Even when there is the surrender of the will to God, with active choice to do His will as it may be revealed, God requires one's cooperation with His Spirit, and the full use of every faculty of the whole man. In short, the powers of darkness aim at obtaining a passive slave, a captive to their will; while God desires a regenerated man who is intelligently and actively both willing and choosing, doing His will in liberation from slavery of spirit, soul and body.

The powers of darkness would make a man a machine, a tool, an automaton; the God of holiness and love desires to make him a free, intelligent sovereign in his own sphere—a thinking, rational, renewed creation created after His own image (Eph. 4:24). Therefore God never says to any faculty of man, "Be thou idle."

God neither needs nor demands *non-activity* in a man for His *working* in and through him; but evil spirits demand the utmost non-activity and passivity.

God asks for intelligent *action* (Rom. 12:1–2, "Your reasonable service") in cooperation with Him.

Satan demands passivity as a condition for his *compulsory* action, and in order compulsorily to subject men to his will and purpose.

God requires the cessation of the *evil actions* of

believers, primarily because they are sinful, and secondly because they hinder cooperation with His Spirit.

Passivity must not be confused with quietness, or the "meek and quiet spirit" which in the sight of God is of great price. Quietness of spirit, of heart, of mind, of manner, voice and expression, may be coexistent with the most effective activity in the will of God (1 Thess. 4:11, mg.: "Be ambitious to be quiet").

There are some who use the word "surrender" and who *think* they are surrendered fully to carry out the will of God but are only so in sentiment and purpose, for actually they walk by the reason and judgment of the natural man, although they submit all their plans to God; and because of this submittal they sincerely believe they are carrying out His will. But those who are really "surrendered" give themselves up implicitly to obey, and carry out at all costs what is revealed to them supernaturally as from God, and not what they themselves plan and reason out to be the will of God.

Believers who surrender their wills and all they are and have to God, yet who WALK BY THE USE OF THEIR NATURAL MINDS, are not the ones who are open to the "passivity" which gives ground to evil spirits—although they may, and do, give ground to them in other ways. The origin of the passivity which gives the evil spirits opportunity to deceive is generally a wrong interpretation of Scripture, or wrong thoughts or beliefs about divine things. Some of these misinterpretations of Scripture, these wrong conceptions which cause men to give way to the passive condition, we have already referred to in a previous chapter.

Such passivity may affect the whole man, in spirit, soul and body, when it has become very deep, and is of many years' standing. But the progress is generally very gradual and insidious in growth, and consequently the release from it is gradual and slow.

PASSIVITY OF THE WILL

There is a *passivity of the will*—the "will" being the helm, so to speak, of the ship. This originates from a wrong conception of what full surrender to God means. Thinking that a "surrendered will" to God means no use of the will at all, the believer ceases to (1) choose, (2) determine, and (3) act of his own volition. (This is very Hindu-like.) Powers of darkness will disguise the seriousness of this, and at first the consequences may seem trivial and be scarcely noticeable. In fact, the initial changes may appear to be glorifying to God. The "strong-willed" person suddenly becomes complacent and yielding—no longer "obnoxious" to his acquaintances. He believes that God is "willing *for* him"—through circumstances and in the decisions of other people—and so he becomes more and more helpless in his actions. After a time no decision can be obtained from him in matters of daily life; no resolve or initiative in matters demanding action. He becomes afraid to express a wish, much less a decision. Others must choose, decide, act, lead, while he drifts as a cork upon the waters. Later on, the powers of darkness begin to make capital out of this "surrendered" believer, and to weave around him various kinds of evil which entangle him through his passivity of will. He has now no power to protest or resist. Conditions which are obviously wrong—springing from things which this believer alone has a right to deal with—flourish, and grow strong and blatant. The powers of darkness have slowly gained because of his passivity of will, which at first was merely submission to his environment under the idea that God was "willing" *for* him in all things around him.

The text that such believers misinterpret is Philippians 2:13, "It is God who worketh in you both to will and to work, for His good pleasure." The "passive" person reads it as "It is God who works in me the willing and the doing," *i.e.*, "God wills *instead of me.*"

The verse actually speaks of God working in the believer's soul up to the point of the action of his will, but the undiscerning reader assumes that God Himself does all the "willing" and the "working." This wrong interpretation justifies his inactivity.

God Does Not Will Instead of Man

The truth to be emphasized is that God never wills INSTEAD of man, and whatever a man does, he is himself responsible for his actions.

The believer whose will has become passive finds, after a time, the greatest difficulty in making decisions of any kind, and he looks outside and all around him for something to help him in deciding the smallest matters. Should he become aware of his passive condition, it is because he has a painful sense of being unable to meet some of the situations of ordinary life. If spoken to, he can hardly listen till a sentence is completed. If asked to judge a matter, he knows he cannot do it. Should he be required to utilize his imagination, he knows he is unable to. He becomes terrified at any proposed course of action where these demands may present themselves. The tactic of the enemy will now be to drive him into situations where these demands will be made, and thus torture or embarrass him before others.

Little does the confused believer realize that in this condition he may, unknowingly, rely upon the *assistance* of evil spirits—the deceivers who have led him into passivity for this very purpose. His unused volitional faculty lies dormant and dead in their grip, but if used it is an occasion for them to manifest themselves through it. They are only too ready to will instead of the man. They will put within his reach many "supernatural" props to help him in any decision—especially Bible texts used apart from their context and "miraculously" given—which the believer, seeking so longingly to do the will of God, seizes upon, and firmly grasps as a drowning man does a rope. By this apparently "divinely given" help he is further blinded to the principle that God only works through the active volition of a man, and not instead of him in matters requiring his action.

PASSIVITY OF THE MIND

Passivity of the mind is a condition engendered by a wrong concept of the important place of the mind in the life surrendered to God: for obeying Him in the Holy Spirit. Christ's calling out of fishermen—common, unschooled laborers—has been sometimes used as an excuse for not cultivating the power of one's brain. Yes, some believers say God has no use for an educated brain, and can do without it! But the choice of Paul, who had the greatest intellect of his age, shows that when God sought for a man through whom He could lay the foundations of the Church, He chose one with a mind capable of vast and intelligent thinking. The greater the brain power, the greater the use God can make of it, provided it is submissive to truth. True, the cause of passivity of mind sometimes lies in the thought that the working of the intellect is a hindrance to the development of the divine life in the believer. But the fact is, that (1) the non-working of the brain hinders, (2) the evil working of the brain hinders, (3) but the normal and pure working of the brain is essential and helpful for cooperation with God.

The effect of passivity of the mind is usually seen in inactivity when there should be action, but it may also be seen in over-activity beyond control—as if a suddenly released instrument broke forth into ungovernable action. It can result also in hesitation, rashness, indecision, unwatchfulness, lack of concentration, lack of judgment, and bad memory.

Passivity does not change the nature of a faculty but it hinders its normal operation. In the case of passivity hindering the memory, the person will be found looking outside himself for every possible "aid to memory" until he becomes a veritable slave to notebook and helps, which may fail at a critical moment. With this comes also passivity of the imagination, which places the imagination outside personal control and at the mercy of evil spirits who flash to it what they please. One danger is to take these visions and *call them "imaginations."*

This passive state can be produced without stooping to crystal gazing. "Crystal gazing" is the practice of staring into a crystal ball or similar object for a prolonged period; the natural vision is dulled, and deceiving spirits can then present anything to the mind.

In pure inactivity of the mind, the mind can be used at the will of the person, but in evil passivity of the mind the person is helpless, and he "can't think!" He feels as if his mind were bound and held by an iron band, or by a weight or pressure on his head.

Passivity of Judgment and Reason

Passivity of judgment and reason: the man in this condition has closed his mind to all arguments and clarifying statements. He has come to settled conclusions; all attempts to give him further truth and light are rejected as interference, while the person attempting it is regarded as ignorant or intrusive. God's expressed will, given in words spoken "supernaturally" to him, has become his law, so that he cannot be induced to reason about it. The believer in this stage of passivity lapses into a state of evil positiveness and infallibility, from which nothing can release him except the rude shock of seeing that he has been deceived by evil spirits. Undermining the deception of a believer in this condition almost means the re-laying of the very foundations of his spiritual life. Hence the very few—called "fanatics" and "cranks" by the world—who have been saved out of this degree of the deception of the enemy.

Passivity of the Conscience

Passivity of the reasoning powers leads naturally to what may be described as *passivity of the conscience.* The conscience becomes passive through non-use when believers think that they are being guided by a higher law of being told to do this or that directly from God; that is, by direct guidance through voices and texts.

When believers sink into passivity of conscience there is, in some cases, a manifestation of moral degradation, and in others stagnation, or retrogression in life or service. Rather than using either mind or conscience in deciding what is right and what is wrong, they say they walk according to the "voice of God." This they make the deciding factor in all their decisions. When they "hear God" they will not listen to their reason or conscience, nor to the words of others; for having come to a decision through the supposed direction of God, their minds become as a closed and sealed book on the matter in question.

In actual fact, having ceased to use their true reasoning powers they become open to all kinds of suggestions from evil spirits. For example, in regard to the coming of Christ: some have falsely reasoned that because Christ is coming very soon (perhaps on a date revealed to them) they do not need to carry on their usual work, overlooking the words of the Lord on this very matter: "Who then is the faithful and *wise* servant, whom his lord hath set over his household, to give them their food in due season? Blessed is that servant, whom his lord when he cometh shall find so doing" (Matt. 24:45–46).

Because of what he will gain through it, the devil will do anything to engender passivity in any form whatsoever, in spirit or mind or body.

PASSIVITY OF THE SPIRIT

Passivity of the spirit is closely associated with passivity of mind, because there is a vital relationship between mind and spirit: a wrong thought generally reveals a wrong spirit, and a wrong spirit engenders a wrong thought.

This form of passivity may come about through:

(1) Ignorance of the laws of the spirit—especially, how to maintain the freedom of the spirit.

(2) Wrong mental conclusions. Mixing up feelings—the physical, soulish and spiritual—not knowing which is which: *i.e.*, (*a*) putting the spiritual down to soulish or physical, or (*b*) attributing to the spiritual that which is natural and physical.

(3) Depending upon the soulish life instead of the spiritual, through lack of knowledge of the difference between them. Also, by quenching one's spirit through ignoring the spiritual sense—for the mind should be able to read "the sense of the spirit" as clearly as it does the senses of seeing, hearing, smelling, and all other senses of the body. There is a knowledge by the mind and a knowledge by the spirit; hence a "sense" of the spirit, which we should learn to understand. It should be read, used, cultivated, and when there is a weight on the spirit of the believer he should be able to recognize it and know how to get rid of it.

(4) Drainage and exhaustion of the body or mind, by constant activity or excessive use. In short, the mind and body must be released from strain before the spirit can be fully operative. (Note the experience of Elijah in 1 Kings 19:4–5, 8–9a.)

Worrying over the past or about the future checks the free action of the spirit by making the outer man and outer affairs dominant, instead of the inner man being at liberty for the will of God at each moment.

When one violates or ignores these important precepts, the spirit becomes locked up, so to speak, so that it cannot act. The rapidity with which a believer can then sink into passivity, as he will at any moment when the resisting attitude ceases, may be likened to the sinking of a stone in water.

PASSIVITY OF THE BODY

When *passivity of body* takes place it practically means a cessation of conscious action, because this passivity affects sight, hearing, smell, taste, feeling, etc. Any person in normal health should be able to focus his eyes on whatever object he chooses, randomly or by design, and should have similar control over all his other senses. They all are avenues of information for his mind and spirit. But when any of these senses are kept in a passive state, consciousness becomes dulled and deadened. Such a person, unaware of what he should be keenly alive to, becomes mechanical in his actions. Peculiar or even repulsive habits easily take hold. It is much simpler for persons in this condition to see these flaws in others than to recognize what is going on in themselves, even though they may be fully aware of external influences which affect them.

When this passive condition brought about by evil spirits reaches its climax, passivity of other parts of the body may result, such as stiff fingers, lost elasticity of the frame in walking, lethargy, heaviness, stooping of the back and spine. The handshake is flabby and passive; the eyes will not look straight into the eyes of others, but move from side to side—all indicating passivity, brought about by deepening interference of the powers of darkness with the whole man, *resulting from the initial passive condition of the will and mind,* in which the man gave up (1) his self-control, and (2) use of his will.

PASSIVITY OF THE WHOLE MAN

At this stage every department of the whole being is

affected. The man acts without using, or using fully, the mind, will, imagination, reason; that is, without thinking (volitionally), deciding, imagining, reasoning. The affections seem dormant, as well as all the faculties of mind and body. In some cases the bodily needs are also dormant, or else the man suppresses them, and deprives himself of food, sleep, and bodily comfort at the dictation of the spirits in control, thus carrying out a "severity to the body" which is not of any real value against the indulgence of the flesh (Col. 2:23). The animal part of the man may also be awakened, and while stoical in sensibilities and feeling he becomes gluttonous in the demand for supply of bodily needs; that is, the machinery of the bodily frame goes on working independently of the control of mind or will, for the body now dominates spirit and soul. Men may live (1) in the human spirit, (2) in the soul, or (3) in the body; for example, the glutton lives in, or after, the body; the student, in mind or soul; the spiritual man, "in the spirit."

(But don't be misled by names. "Spiritists" are not really true men of spirit—for they live in the sense realm generally, and have to do with "spirit" only through their dealing with the evil spiritual forces, through understanding the laws for their workings and fulfilling them.)

The Spirit Sense Lost in Sensations of the Body

When the believer is in any degree deceived by evil spirits, he is liable to live in the body, give way to the sensuous, and to be dominated by the physical realm. This can become the case through "spiritual" experiences felt in the physical frame, but which are not really spiritual because not from the Spirit. A sense of "fire" in the body, "glow," "thrills," and all exquisite bodily sensations from apparently "spiritual" causes, really *feed the senses;* and, unconsciously to themselves, while they have these experiences, such believers live in the sense-realm, practically walking "after the flesh," *though they call themselves "spiritual."* For this reason "I keep under my body, and bring it into subjection" (1 Cor. 9:27, KJV) *is practically impossible* in this state of deception, because the sense-life is aroused in all kinds of ways, and the sensations of the body are forced upon the consciousness of the man. *The spirit sense is practically lost in the acute realization of all the sensations in the bodily consciousness.*

May I point out that a man in normal health is oblivious of the physical action of breathing going on in his physical frame. In like manner, a believer under the domination of the Spirit ceases to register his bodily sensations; but the opposite is the case when evil spirits have awakened the sense-life to abnormal action, either by beautiful experiences or the contrary.

The cultivation of this condition of passivity may be ignorantly and sedulously carried out for years by the surrendered believer, so that it deepens its hold upon him to an incredible extent; until, when it reaches its consummation, the man may become so under the bondage of it as to awaken suddenly to his state. But then he may think that "natural causes" alone explain his condition, or else, in some unaccountable way, his acute sensitiveness to God and divine things has become dulled beyond power of restoration or renewal. The physical feelings become deadened or atrophied, and the affections seem petrified and stoical. This is the time when deceiving spirits suggest that he has grieved God beyond repair, and the man goes through agonies of seeking the Presence he thinks he has grieved away.

The cultivation of passivity may come about from reliance upon the many helps contrived (unknowingly) by the person to counteract or obviate the inconvenience of the passive state, such as the provision of and dependence upon outward helps to the eye for assisting the passive memory, utterance in speech to assist the "thinking" of the passive mind, and what may be termed "crutches" of all kinds, known only to the individual—elaborately constructed, and multiplied to meet his particular needs, but all keeping him from recognizing his true condition, even if he has the knowledge for doing so.

Manifestations of Influence of Evil Spirits Called Natural Idiosyncrasies

But this truth about the working of evil spirits among believers, and the causes and symptoms of their power upon mind or body, has been so veiled in ignorance that multitudes are deceived by them. The manifestations are generally taken as natural idiosyncrasies or infirmities. The Lord's work is put on one side, or even never taken up, because the believer is "over-strained," or else "without gifts" for doing it. He is "nervous," "timid," has "no gift of speech, no power of thought" where the service of God is concerned; but in the social sphere these "deficiencies" are forgotten, and the timid ones shine out at their best. It does not occur to them to ask why it is that only in God's service are they thus incapable. But it is only in respect to such a service that the hidden workings of Satan interfere.

The Shock When the Believer Apprehends the Truth

The shock is great when the believer first apprehends the truth of deception as possible for himself; but as the ultimate issue is realized, the joy of the one who sets himself to understand and fight through to full deliverance is more than words can tell. Light pours in upon the unsolved problems of years, in both his personal experience and in the perplexities surrounding him, as well as on conditions in the Church and in the world.

As he seeks for light from God, the subtle inroads of the deceiving spirits into his life slowly become clear to the open-minded believer; and their many devices to deceive him stand revealed as the searchlight of truth goes far back into the past, uncovering the cause of unaccountable difficulties in experience and life, and many mysterious happenings which had been accepted as "the inscrutable will of God."

PASSIVITY! How many have fallen into it, little knowing their state! Through the misuse of their faculties much time is lost in dependence upon the help of outward circumstances and environment. In the lives of so many there is much "doing," with so little accomplished . . . many beginnings, and few endings. How familiar we are with the words, "Yes, I can do that," and the impulse is there, but by the time the need for action has come the passive man has lost his momentary interest. This is the key to much of the lamented "apathy" and the dulled sympathy of Christians to really spiritual things, while they are keenly alive to the social or worldly elements around them. The worldling can be stirred in acutest feeling for the sufferings of others, but many of the children of God have, unknowingly, opened themselves to a supernatural power which has dulled them in thought and mind and sympathy. Ever craving for comfort and happiness and peace in spiritual things, they have sung themselves into a "passivity"—*i.e.*, a passive state of "rest," "peace" and "joy"—which has given opportunity to the powers of darkness to lock them up in the prison of themselves, and thus make them incapable of sensitively understanding the needs of a suffering world.

PASSIVITY OCCASIONED BY WRONG INTERPRETATIONS OF THE TRUTH OF "DEATH"

This condition of passivity may come about by wrong

interpretations of truth, even the truth of "death with Christ" as set forth in Romans 6 and Galatians 2:20, when it is carried beyond the true balance of the Word of God. God calls upon true believers to reckon themselves "dead indeed unto sin," and also to the evil self-life, even in a religious or "holiness" form; *that is, the life which came from the first Adam, the old creation.* But this does not mean a death to the human personality, for Paul said, "Yet I live," although "Christ liveth in me!" There is a retention of the personal being, the ego, the will, the personality, which is to be dominated by the Spirit of God as He energizes the man's individuality, held by him in "self-control" (Gal. 5:23, mg.).

In light of the misunderstanding of the truth of "death with Christ"—conceived to mean passivity, and suppression of the actions of the personality of the man—it is now easy to see why the proclamation of the truths connected with Romans 6:6 and Galatians 2:20 have been the prelude, in some cases, to *supernatural manifestations of the powers of darkness.* The believer, through the misunderstanding of these truths, is actually fulfilling the primary conditions for the working of evil spirits, the very conditions understood by spiritist mediums to be necessary for obtaining the manifestations they desire. In such cases it may be said that truth is the devil's fulcrum for launching his lies.

So far as Romans 6 is understood to be a *present moment* declaration of an attitude to sin, and Galatians 2:20 a similar declaration of an attitude toward God—and 2 Corinthians 4:10–12 and Philippians 3:10 the outworking of the Spirit of God in bringing the believer into actual conformity to the death of Christ as he maintains his declared attitude—the powers of darkness are defeated; for this "here-and-now" declared attitude demands *active volition, active cooperation* with the Risen Lord, and *active acceptance* of the path of the cross. But when these truths are interpreted to mean (1) a loss of personality; (2) an absence of volition and self-control, and (3) the passive letting go of the "I myself" into a condition of machine-like, blind, automatic "obedience," with deadness and heaviness which the believer thinks is "mortification" or "the working of death" in him, it makes the truth of death with Christ a fulfilling of conditions for evil spirits to work, and removes the conditions in which God can alone work. So "supernatural manifestations" taking place on the *basis of passivity* can have no other source than the *lying spirits*, however beautiful and God-like they may be.

This counterfeit of spiritual "death" may take place in regard to spirit, soul or body. How the truth of death with Christ can be misconstrued, and made the occasion for evil spirits to obtain the ground of passivity, may be exampled in some of the following ways:

Misconception of Self-Effacement

1. *Passivity caused by misconception of self-effacement.* Under the idea that surrender of self to God means self-effacement, self-renunciation, and, practically, self-annihilation, the believer has aimed at unconsciousness of (*a*) personality, (*b*) personal needs, (*c*) personal states, feelings, desires, external appearance, circumstances, discomforts, opinions of others, etc., so as to be "conscious" of God *only* moving, working, acting, through him. To this end he has given over his "self-consciousness" to "death" and has prayed that he might have no consciousness of anything in the world but the presence of God. Then, to carry out this absolute surrender of self to death—this entire self-effacement—he consistently, in practice, "yields to death" every trace of the movement of "self" he becomes aware of, and sets his will steadily to renounce all consciousness of personal wishes, desires, tastes, needs, feelings, etc. All this—appearing to be so "self-sacrificing"

and "spiritual"—results in an entire suppression of personality, and the giving of ground to evil spirits in a passivity of the whole being. This permits the powers of darkness to work, and bring about an "unconsciousness" which becomes in time a deadness and dullness of the sensibilities, and an inability to feel—not only for himself but for others, so as not to know when they suffer or when he himself causes suffering.

MISCONCEPTION OF TRUTH PART OF "TEACHINGS" OF DECEIVING SPIRITS

As this conception of self-effacement and loss of self-consciousness is contrary to the believer's full use of the faculties which the Spirit of God requires for cooperation with Him, evil spirits gain ground on the basis of this deception about "death." The *misconception* of what death means in practice was really part of their "teachings," subtly suggested, and received by the man who was ignorant of the possibility of deception over what looked like devoted, whole-hearted surrender to God. The "teachings of demons" can, therefore, be based on truth.

The effect of the deception on the believer is, in due time, an insensitivity *produced by evil spirits* which is hard to break. In his state of insensitiveness he has no ability to discern, recognize, feel or know things around him, or in himself. He is unaware of his actions, ways and manners, together with a hyper-self-consciousness which he is not conscious of, and which makes him easily hurt but unaware of his own hurting of others. He has practically become stoical, and unable to see the effect of his actions in putting others into suffering. He acts without volitional thinking, reasoning, imagining, or deciding what he says and does. His actions are mechanical and automatic. He is unconscious of sometimes being a channel for the transmission of words, thoughts, or feelings which pass through him apart from the action of his will and his knowledge of the source.

Passivity Caused by Wrong Acceptance of Suffering

2. *Passivity caused by wrong acceptance of suffering.* The believer consents to accept "suffering with Christ" in "the way of the cross." To fulfill this surrender he *passively yields to suffering* in whatever form it may come, believing that "suffering with Christ" means (*a*) reward, and (*b*) fruitfulness. He does not know that evil spirits can produce counterfeit "suffering," and that he may be accepting suffering from them though believing it to be from the hand of God, and, by so doing, giving ground to them. And what does he consider "suffering" to be? Both sin in the life which cannot be got rid of, and suffering in the life which cannot be explained. By recognizing the truth of deception the first can be got rid of, and the latter explained.

Suffering is an obvious factor in motivating a person to take a certain course. So it is a great weapon for evil spirits to use in controlling men, for by suffering they can drive a man to do what he would not do otherwise. Not realizing this, the believer may entirely misinterpret the suffering he goes through. Believers are often deceived over what they think to be their "vicarious" suffering for others, perhaps even for the Church as a whole. They look upon themselves as martyrs when they are really victims, unaware that "suffering" is one of the chief symptoms of deception. By putting a man into suffering, the evil spirits gleefully ease themselves of their enmity and hatred to man.

Marks of Suffering Caused by Evil Spirits

Suffering directly caused by evil spirits may be distinguished from the true fellowship of Christ's sufferings by its complete absence of *result*, either in fruit, victory, or ripening in spiritual growth. If carefully observed, it will be seen to be entirely purposeless. God does nothing without a definite object. He does not delight in causing suffering for the sake of suffering, but the devil does. Suffering caused by evil spirits is acute and fiendish in its character, and there will be no *inward witness of the Spirit* which tells the suffering believer that it is from the hand of God. To a discerning eye it can be as clearly diagnosed to be from an evil spirit as can any physical pain be distinguished from a mental one by a skillful physician.

The suffering caused by evil spirits can be (1) *spiritual*, causing acute suffering in the spirit—injecting "feelings" into the spirit, repugnant or poignant; (2) *soulish*, producing acute darkness, confusion, chaos, horror in the mind—anguished, knifelike emotional pain; or (3) *physical:* pain in any part of the body.

The ground given for the evil spirits to produce counterfeit suffering in such an acute degree as this may be traced back to the time when the believer, in his absolute surrender to God for "the way of the cross," deliberately willed to *accept suffering from Him*. Then afterwards, in fulfillment of this surrender, he gave ground to the enemy: by accepting some specific suffering as from God which *really came from the spirits of evil*, thus opening the door to them, by (1) the reception of their lie, (2) the admittance of their actual power manifested in the suffering—continuing still further to give more ground by believing *their* interpretation of the suffering—and (3) doing so as "the will of God"; until the whole life became one prolonged "yielding to suffering," which seemed unreasonable, unaccountable in its origin, and purposeless in its results. God's character is thus often maligned to His children, and the deceiving spirits do their utmost to arouse rebellion against Him *for what they themselves are doing.*

Passivity Through Wrong Ideas of Humility

3. *Passivity caused by wrong ideas of humility and self-abasement.* The believer consents, when accepting

"death," to let it be carried out in a "nothingness" and a "self-effacement" which gives him no place for proper and true self-estimation whatsoever. (Contrast this with 2 Cor. 10:12–18.) If the believer accepts the self-depreciation *suggested to him and created by evil spirits*, it brings an atmosphere of hopelessness and weakness about him, and he conveys to others a spirit of darkness and heaviness, sadness and grief. His spirit is easily crushed, wounded and depressed. He may attribute the cause to "sin," without being aware of any specific sin in his life; or he may even look upon his "suffering" experience as "vicarious" suffering for the Church. But an abnormal sense of suffering is one of the chief symptoms of deception.

In contrast to the true elimination of pride and all the forms of sin arising from it, the counterfeit caused by deception may be recognized by (1) the believer obtruding his self-depreciation at moments most inopportune, with painful perplexity to those who hear it; (2) a shrinking back from service for God, with inability to recognize the interests of the kingdom of Christ; (3) a laborious effort to keep "I" out of sight, both in conversation and action, and yet which forces the "I" more into view in an objectionable form; (4) a deprecatory, apologizing manner, which gives opportunity to the "world-rulers of the darkness of this world" to instigate their subjects to crush and put aside this "not I" person, at moments of strategic importance to the kingdom of God; (5) an atmosphere around such a one of weakness, darkness, sadness, grief, lack of hope, easily wounded touchiness. All these may be the result of a believer "willing," in some moment of "surrender to death," to accept an effacement of his true personality—but which God requires as a vessel for the manifestation of the Spirit of God, in a life of fullest cooperation with the Spirit of God. This believer, by his wrong belief and submission to evil spirits, suppressed into passivity a personality which could not and was not meant to "die"; and by this passivity he played into the hands of the powers of darkness.

Passivity Caused by Wrong Thoughts About Weakness

4. *Passivity caused by a wrong thought about weakness.* The believer consents to a perpetual condition of weakness, under a false conception that it is a necessary state for the manifestation of divine life and strength. This is generally based upon Paul's words, "When I am weak, then am I strong." The believer needs to apprehend that this was a statement made by the apostle of a simple fact that when he was weak, he found God's strength sufficient for accomplishing His will—and that it is not an exhortation to God's children deliberately to *will* to be weak. This would make a person unfit for service in many ways. Instead, one should say, "I can do all things through Christ who strengtheneth me." That "willing to be weak" so as to "have a claim on Christ's strength" is a wrong attitude can readily be seen. Such a "weakness" is not in accord with God's plan and provision. It actually hinders God's strengthening; and by this subtle deception of the enemy in the minds of many, God is robbed of much active service for Him.

Passivity with Satanic Activity

This statement in 2 Corinthians 12:10 must not be twisted so as to teach "passivity." For once the man becomes passive in volition and mind, he is held by deceiving spirits without power to act, or is driven into satanic *activity*—uncontrollable activity of thought, restlessness of body, and wild, unbalanced action of all degrees. The actions are spasmodic and intermittent, the person sometimes dashing ahead and at other times being sluggish and slow—like a machine in a factory with the wheels whirring aimlessly, because the switch at the control center is out of the hand of the master. The man cannot work, even when he sees so much to be done, and is feverish because he cannot do it. During the time of passivity he appeared to be content, but when he is driven into satanic activity he is restless and out of accord with all things around him. Though his environment should lead him to a state of full contentment, yet something (may it not be "somebody"?) makes it impossible for him to be in harmony with his external circumstances, however pleasant they may be. He is conscious of a restlessness and activity which is painfully feverish; or else of passivity and weight, of a doing of "work" and yet no work. All these are manifestations of a demoniacal destruction of one's peace.

DELIVERANCE FROM PASSIVITY

The believer needing deliverance from the condition of passivity must first seek to understand what should be his normal or right condition, and then test or examine himself in the light of it to discern if evil spirits have been interfering. To do this, let him recollect a moment in his life which he would call his "best"—either in spirit, soul and body, or in his whole being—and then let him look upon this as his normal condition, one which he would want to be maintained, and never rest satisfied below it.

Since the passivity has come about gradually it can only end gradually, as it is detected and destroyed. The full cooperation of the man is necessary for its removal—a major reason for the long period needed for deliverance. Deception and passivity can only be removed as the man *understands*, and cooperates by the use of his volition in the refusal of both the deception and the ground upon which it was based.

It is important to keep perpetually in mind the standard of the normal condition, and should at any time the believer drop below it, to find out the cause, so as to have it removed. Whatever faculty or part of one's being has been surrendered into passivity, and therefore lost for use, must be retaken by the active exercise of the will, and thus brought back into personal control. The ground which had been given—which caused the fall into bondage to the enemy—must be eliminated and then refused persistently, in a steady resistance to the spirits of evil in their hold of it. Remember, the powers of darkness will fight against the loss of any part of their kingdom in man, just as any earthly government would fight to protect its own territory and subjects. But the "Stronger than he" is the Conqueror, and will strengthen the believer for the battle and full recovery of the spoil.

CHAPTER 5

COUNTERFEITS OF THE DIVINE

In seeking to deceive the believer, the first great effort of evil spirits is directed toward getting him to accept their suggestions and workings as being the speaking, working, or leading of God. Their initial device is to counterfeit a "Divine Presence," under cover of which they can mislead their victim as they wish. Remember, the word "counterfeit" means THE SUBSTITUTION OF THE FALSE FOR THE TRUE.

The condition on the part of the believer which gives the deceiving spirits their opportunity is sometimes a mistaken belief regarding the location of God. God is present either (1) in them (consciously), or (2) around them (consciously). When they pray they think of and pray to God in themselves, or else to God around them—in the room or atmosphere. They use their imagination, and try to "realize" His presence, and they desire to "feel" His presence in them or upon them.

THE MISLOCATION OF GOD BY THE BELIEVERS

This locating of God in or around the believer usually comes about at the time of some special crisis in one's life, before which he lived more by the acceptance of facts declared in the Scriptures, as understood by his intelligence. But then he becomes more "conscious" of the presence of God by the Spirit and in the spirit, and so begins to locate the Person of God as in, around, or upon him. So he turns inward, and begins to pray to

God as within him—which in time may even result in prayer to evil spirits.

The logical sequence of prayer to God as located within can be pressed to absurdity, *i.e.*, if a person can pray to God residing in himself, why not pray to God in another, elsewhere? The possible dangers arising from this misconception of truth—the subjectivizing of God as a Person within—are obvious.

Some believers live so inwardly in communion, worship and vision as to become spiritually introverted, and cramped and narrowed in their outlook; with the result that their spiritual capacity and mental powers become dwarfed and powerless. Others become victims to the "inner voice" and the introverted attitude of listening to it—which is the ultimate result of the location of God as a Person within—so that eventually the mind becomes fixed in the introverted condition with no out-going action at all.

In fact, all turning inwards to a subjective location of God as indwelling, speaking, communing and guiding—in a materialistic or conscious sense—is open to gravest danger; for upon this thought and belief, sedulously cultivated by the powers of darkness, the most serious deceptions of deceiving spirits have taken place.

The Ultimate Result of a Mistaken Location of God

From this mistaken idea about the location of God—used by evil spirits as the groundwork for manifestations which seem to support this concept—have come about the delusions of believers during past ages, and in recent years, who assert themselves to *be* "Christ." On the same premise will come about the great deceptions at the end of the age, foretold by the Lord in Matthew 24:24, of the "false Christs" and false prophets; and the "I am the Christ" claim by leaders of groups of side-tracked believers, and the thousands of others who have been sent to asylums even though not truly monomaniacs. The devil's richest harvest is from the effects of his counterfeits; and unwittingly, many sober and faithful teachers of "holiness" have aided him in his deceptions through the use of language which gives a materialistic idea of spiritual things, and which is eagerly laid hold of by the natural mind.

Those who locate God personally and wholly in themselves make themselves, by their assertions, practically "divine" persons. God is not wholly in any man. He dwells in those who receive Him, by His own Spirit communicated to them. "God is Spirit," and mind or body cannot hold communion with spirit. Sensuous feelings, or "conscious" physical enjoyment of some supposed spiritual presence, is not true communion of spirit with Spirit, such as the Father seeks from those who worship Him (John 4:24).

God is in heaven. Christ the Glorified Man is in heaven. The location of the God we worship is of supreme importance. If we think of our God as in us, and around us, for our worship and for our "enjoyment," we unwittingly open the door to the evil spirits in the atmosphere which surrounds us—instead of our penetrating in spirit through the lower heavens (see Heb. 4:14; 9:24; 10:19–20) to the throne of God, which is in the highest heaven, "above all principality and power, . . . and every name that is named, not only in this world, but also in that which is to come" (Eph. 1:21, KJV).

THE TRUE LOCATION OF GOD

The Word of God is very clear on this point, and we need only ponder such passages as Hebrews 1:3; 2:9, 4:14–16, 9:24, and many others, to see it. The God we worship, the Christ we love, is in heaven. It is as we approach Him there, and by faith apprehend our union with Him in spirit there, that we are raised with Him above the plane of the lower heavens where the powers of darkness reign and, seated with Him, see them under His feet (Eph. 1:20–23, 2:6).

The Lord's words recorded in the Gospel of John, chapters 14, 15, and 16, give the truth very clearly concerning His indwelling the believer. The "in Me" speaks of being with Him in His heavenly position (John 14:20)—the result of the believer's faith in Him; and the "I in you"—spoken to the company of disciples, and hence to the Body of Christ as a whole—follows as a result in the life of the individual believer. This union with the Person in the glory results in the inflow and outflow of His Spirit and life through the believer on earth (see Phil. 1:19). In other words, *the "subjective" is the result of the "objective."* The fact that Christ is in heaven is the basis of faith for the subjective inflow of His life and power by the Holy Spirit of God.

Christ as a Person in Heaven

The Lord said, "If ye abide in Me [*i.e.*, in the glory], and My words abide in you, ask whatsoever ye will . . ." (John 15:7). Christ abides in us by His Spirit, and *through His words*, but He Himself, as a Person, is in heaven, and it is only as we abide in Him there that His Spirit and His life, through His Word, can be manifested in us here.

"Abiding" means an attitude of trust and dependence on Him in heaven; but if one's attitude is changed into a trust and dependence upon a Christ within, it is really a resting upon an inward experience and *a turning from the Christ in heaven.* This actually blocks the avenue for the inflow of His life, and disassociates the believer from cooperation with Him by the Spirit. Any manifestation, therefore, of a "presence" within cannot be a true "manifestation" from God if it uncenters the believer from his right attitude toward the Christ in heaven.

There is a true knowledge of the presence of God, but

it is *in the spirit*, when joined to Him who is within the veil—a knowledge of spiritual union and fellowship with Him which lifts the believer, so to speak, out of himself to abide with Christ in God.

The counterfeit "presence" of God is nearly always manifested in the guise of love, to which the believer opens himself without hesitation. He may find that it fills and satiates his innermost being; but being deceived, he does not know that he has opened himself to the activity of evil spirits.

THE COUNTERFEIT PRESENCE OF GOD

How the powers of darkness counterfeit the presence of God to those ignorant of their devices may be somewhat as follows. At some moment when the believer is yearning for the *sense* of God's presence, either alone or in a meeting, and certain conditions are fulfilled, the subtle foe approaches, and wrapping the *senses* round with a soothing, lulling feeling—sometimes filling the room with light, or causing what is apparently a "breath from God" by a movement of the air—either whispers, "This is the presence you have longed for," or leads the believer to infer that it is what he has desired.

Then, off his guard, and lulled into security that Satan is far away, some thoughts are suggested to the mind, accompanied by manifestations which appear to be divine. A sweet voice speaks, or a vision is given, which is at once received as "divine guidance," given in the "divine presence," and hence beyond question as from God. If accepted as from God *when actually from the spirits of evil*, the first ground is gained.

The man is now sure that God has bidden him do this or that. He is filled with the thought that he has been highly favored of God and chosen for some high place in His Kingdom. The deeply hidden self-love is fed and strengthened by this, and he is able to endure all things by the power of this secret strength. He has been spoken to by God! He has been singled out for special favor! *His support is now within—based upon his experience—rather than established upon God Himself and the written Word.* Through this secret confidence that God has specially spoken to him, the man becomes unteachable and unyielding, with a positiveness trending on infallibility. He cannot listen to others now, for they have not had this "direct" revelation from God. He is in direct, special, personal communion with God, and to question any "direction" given to him becomes the height of sin. Obey he must, even though the direction given is contrary to all enlightened judgment and the action commanded is opposed to the spirit of the Word of God. In brief, when the man at this stage believes he has a "command" from God he will not use his reason, because he thinks it would be "carnal" to do so. "Common sense" is lack of faith, and therefore sin; and "conscience," for the time being, has ceased to speak.

Some of the suggestions made to the believer by deceiving spirits at this time may be: (1) *"You are a special instrument for God"*—working to feed self-love; (2) *"You are more advanced than others"*—working to blind the soul to sober knowledge of itself; (3) *"You are different from others"*—working to make him think he needs special dealing by God; (4) *"You must take a separate path"*—a suggestion made to feed the independent spirit; (5) *"You must give up your occupation and live by faith"*—aiming at causing the believer to launch out on false guidance, which may result in the ruin of his home, and sometimes the work for God in which he is engaged.

All these suggestions are made to give the man a false concept of his spiritual state; for he is made to believe he is more advanced than he actually is, so that he may act beyond his measure of faith and knowledge (Rom.12:3), and consequently be more open to the deceptions of the beguiling foe.

The Counterfeit Presence Is Sensuous

Counterfeits of the Father, the Son and the Holy Spirit are recognizable by the manifestations being given to the senses, *i.e.*, in the physical realm. For the true indwelling of God is in the shrine of the spirit alone; and the soul vessel, or personality of the believer, is purely a vehicle for the *expression* of Christ, who is enthroned within by His Spirit; while the body, quickened by the same Spirit, is governed by God from the central depths of the human spirit, through the self-control of the man acting by his renewed will.

The counterfeit presence of God is given by deceiving spirits working upon the physical frame, or within the bodily frame but upon the senses. We have seen the beginning of this, and how the first ground is gained. Control is advanced by these sense-manifestations being repeated, ever so gently, so that the man goes on yielding to them, thinking this is truly "communion with God"—for believers too often look upon communion with God as a thing of sense, rather than of spirit. So he starts praying to evil spirits under the belief that he is praying to God. The self-control is not yet lost, but as the believer responds to or gives himself up to these "conscious" manifestations, he does not realize that his will power is being slowly undermined. At last, through these subtle, delicious experiences, a conviction is established that *God Himself is in possession of the body*, quickening it with felt thrills of life, or filling it with warmth and heat, or even with "agonies" which seem like fellowship with the sufferings of Christ and His travail for souls, or the experience of death with Christ in the consciousness of nails being driven into the bodily frame, etc. From this point the lying spirits can work as they will, and there is no limit as to what they may do to one who is deceived to this extent.

Counterfeit manifestations of the divine life in various modes now follow quickly: movements in the body, pleasant thrills, touches, a glow as of fire in different parts of the body; or sensations of cold, shakings and tremblings—all of which are accepted as from God.

Evil spirits work by sudden suggestion—which is not the ordinary working of the mind but suggestions which come from without—"flashes of memory," again not the ordinary working of the memory but thoughts coming from without; touches and twitches of the nerves; feelings of a draft and sensations of wind blowing upon the area round about, etc.

Compulsory "Confessions" of Sin

Evil spirits may push a person to painful public confessions of wrongdoing, which he hopes will result in his regaining an "experience" apparently lost; but all in vain. These confessions instigated by deceiving spirits may be recognized by their compulsory character. The man is *forced* to "confess" sin—and ofttimes sins which have no existence, except in the accusations of the enemy. As it does not dawn upon him that evil spirits will drive a man to do what looks like a most meritorious thing, and which the Scriptures declare is the one condition for obtaining forgiveness, he yields to the pressure upon him, simply to get relief. Herein lies the danger of widespread "confessions of sin" during times of revival, when a veritable "wave" of confession passes over a community, and the depths of sinful lives are exposed to the gaze of others. This enables the lying spirits to disseminate the very poison of the pit into the atmosphere, and into the minds of the listeners.

True Confession of Sin

True confession of sin should come from deep *conviction* and not compulsion. It should be made only to God, if the sin is one only known by God; to a man personally, and in private, when the sin is against a man; and to the public only when the sin is against the public. Confession should never be made under the impulse of a compelling emotion but should be a deliberate act of the volition—choosing the right and then putting things right, according to the will of God.

That Satan's kingdom gains by public confessions is evident from the devices the enemy uses to push men into them. Evil spirits drive a believer into sin, and then compel that man publicly to confess the sin which they forced him to commit—contrary to his true character—in order to make the sin which they forced him into a stigma upon him for the remainder of his life.

Ofttimes those "sins" confessed have their rise in the believer from the insertion by wicked spirits of feelings as *consciously* abhorrent and loathsome as were the former "conscious" feelings of heavenly purity and love he was experiencing when he declared that he knew of "no sin to confess to God," or "no rising of an evil impulse" whatever—which had led him to believe in the complete elimination of all sin from his being.

In short, the counterfeit manifestations of the divine presence in the body in agreeable and heavenly feelings can be followed by counterfeit feelings of sinful things wholly repugnant to the volition and central purity of the believer—who is as faithful to God now in his hatred to sin as in the days when he revelled in the sense of purity given consciously to his bodily frame.

COUNTFEIT GUIDANCE

Many believers think the "guidance" or "leading" of God to be only by a voice saying "Do this" or "Do that"; or by some compulsory movement or impulse apart from the action or volition of the man. They point to the words used about the Lord: "The Spirit driveth Him into the wilderness." But this was unusual in the life of Christ, for the statement sets the scene for an intense spirit conflict during which the Holy Spirit departed from His ordinary guidance. We have a glimpse into a similar intense movement in the spirit of the Lord Jesus in John 11:33, when, "groaning with indignation in His spirit," He went to the grave of Lazarus. In both instances He was moving forward to a direct conflict with Satan. In the case of Lazarus, it was with Satan as the Prince of Death; the Gethsemane agony was of the same character.

But ordinarily the Lord was guided or led in simple fellowship with the Father: deciding, acting, reasoning, thinking, as One who knew the will of God and intelligently—I speak reverently—carried it out. The "voice" from heaven was rare, and, as the Lord Himself said, was for the sake of others, not for Himself. He knew the Father's will, and with every faculty of His being as man, He did it (see John 4:34, 5:30, 6:38).

As Christ was a pattern or example for His followers, guidance or "leading" in its perfect and true form is shown in His life; and believers can expect the co-working of the Holy Spirit when they walk after the pattern of their Example. Out of line with the Pattern, however, they cease to have the working of the Holy Spirit and become open to the deceptive counterfeit workings of evil spirits.

If the believer ceases to use mind, reason, will, and all his other faculties as a person and depends instead upon voices and impulses for guidance in every detail of life, he will be "led" or guided by evil spirits feigning to be God.

Counterfeit "Inward" Drawings

As his spiritual life develops, the believer knows to a great extent the true guidance of the Spirit of God. He knows true inward constraint to act, and restraint from action in like manner—such as when to speak to another about his soul, when to rise and testify in a meeting, etc. But after a time he may cease to watch for this pure inward moving of the Spirit—often through ignorance of how to read the monitions of his spirit—and may begin to wait for some other incentive or manifestation to guide him in action. This is the time for which the deceiving spirits have been watching. Since at this point the believer has ceased, unknown to himself, to cooperate with the inward spirit action—to use his volition, and to decide for himself—he is now watching for some parallel, supernatural indication of the way to go, or the course to take. Hence he must have "guidance" somehow—some "text," some "indication," some "providential circumstance," etc., etc. This is the moment of opportunity for a deceiving spirit to gain his attention and confidence. And so some words are whispered softly—words that are exactly in accordance with the inward drawing that he has had, but which he does not recognize as from another source. The Holy Spirit, however, led via a deep *inner constraining and restraining of his spirit.* The soft whisper of the deceiving spirit is so delicate and gentle that the believer listens to and receives the words without question, and begins to obey this soft whisper, yielding more and more to it, without any thought of exercising mind, judgment, reason or volition.

The "feelings" are now in the body, but the believer is unaware that he is *ceasing to act from his spirit* and by the pure unfettered action of his will and his mind, which, under the illumination of the Spirit, are always in accord with one's spirit. This is a time of great danger if the believer fails to discriminate the source of his "drawing" feelings and yields to them before finding out. He should examine his basic principle of decision, especially when it has to do with feeling, lest he should be led away by a feeling without being able to say where it comes from and whether it is safe for him to go by it. He should know there are physical feelings, soulish feelings, and feelings in the spirit—any of which can be divine or satanic in their source; therefore reliance on "feelings"—*feeling* drawn, etc.—is a source of great mischief in the Christian life.

From this point deceiving spirits can increase their control, for the believer has begun the listening attitude, which can be developed acutely until he is always watching for an "inner voice" or a voice in the ear, which is an exact counterfeit of the voice of God *in the spirit;* and thus the believer moves and acts as a passive slave to "supernatural guidance."

THE COUNTERFEIT VOICE OF GOD

Evil spirits are able to counterfeit the voice of God because of the ignorance of believers that they can do so, and their ignorance also of the true principle of God's way of communication with His children. The Lord said: "My sheep know My voice . . . ," *i.e.,* My way of speaking to My sheep. He did not say this voice was an *audible* voice, nor a voice giving directions which were to be obeyed apart from the intelligence of the believer; but, on the contrary, the word "know" indicates the use of the mind, for although there is knowledge in the spirit it must reach the intelligence of the man, so that spirit and mind become of one accord.

The question whether God now speaks by *His direct voice* audibly to men needs consideration at this point. A careful study of the epistles of Paul—which contain an exhaustive summation of God's will for the Church, the Body of Christ, even as the books of Moses contained God's will and laws for Israel—seems to make it clear that God, having "spoken to us in His Son," no longer speaks *by His own direct voice* to His people. Nor does it appear that, since the coming of the Holy Spirit to guide the Church of Christ into all truth, He frequently employs angels to speak or to guide His children.

The Ministry of Angels

The angels are "sent forth to minister to the heirs of salvation" (Heb. 1:14, KJV), but not to take the place of Christ or the Holy Spirit. The Apocalypse seems to show that this ministration of angels to the saints on earth is a ministration for war in the spiritual realm against the forces of Satan; but there is little indication given of ministry in any other way. After the first Advent, when there was great angelic activity over the wondrous event of the Father bringing the "Firstborn" of the new race (Rom. 8:29) into the inhabited earth (Heb. 1:6, mg.), and again at the Advent of the Holy Spirit on the Day of Pentecost to begin His work of forming a Body like unto the Risen Head—and during the early years of the Church—the employment of angels in *direct* and *visible communication* with believers seems to give way to the work and ministry of the Holy Spirit.

The entire work of witnessing to Christ, and leading the Church into all truth, has been committed to the Holy Spirit. Therefore all intervention of "angels" or of *audible voices* from the spiritual realm purporting to be from God may be taken as counterfeits of Satan, whose supreme object is to substitute the working of his own wicked spirits in the place of God. In any case, it is best and safest in these days of peril to keep in the path of faith and reliance upon the Holy Spirit of God working through the Word of God.

How to Detect the Source of a Voice

In order to detect which is the "voice of God" and which is the "voice of the devil," we need to understand that the Holy Spirit alone is charged to communicate the will of God to the believer, and that He works from *within the spirit* of the disciple, enlightening the understanding (Eph. 1:17–18) so as to bring him into intelligent co-working with the mind of God.

The purpose of the Holy Spirit is, briefly, the entire renewal of the redeemed one, in spirit, soul and body. He therefore directs all His working to the liberation of every faculty, and never in any way seeks to direct a man as a passive machine, even into *good*. He works in him to enable him to *choose* the good, and strengthens him to act, but never—even for "good"—dulls him or renders him incapable of free action. He would nullify the very purpose of Christ's redemption on Calvary, and the purpose of His own coming.

When believers understand these principles, the "voice of the devil" is recognizable: (1) when it comes from outside the man, or within the sphere of his perception, and not from the central depth of his spirit where the Holy Spirit abides; (2) *when it is imperative and persistent, urging sudden action without time to reason or intelligently weigh the issues;* (3) when it is confusing and clamorous, so that the man is hindered from thinking. For the Holy Spirit desires the believer to be intelligent, as a responsible being with a choice, and will not confuse him so as to make him incapable of coming to a decision.

The speaking of evil spirits can also be a counterfeit of the apparent inner speaking of the man himself, as if he were himself "thinking," and yet with no concentrated action of the mind; *e.g.*, a persistent and ceaseless "commentary" going on somewhere within, apart from volition or mind action, commenting on the man's own actions or the actions of others, such as "You are wrong," "You are never right," "God has cast you off," "You must not do that," etc., etc.

How to Detect the Source of "Texts" Supernaturally Spoken

The "voice of the devil" as an angel of light is more difficult to detect when it comes with wonderful strings of texts which makes it appear like the voice of the Holy

Spirit. Voices from without, either as from God or angels, may be rejected, yet the believer may be deceived by "floods of texts" which he thinks are from God. So the detection requires further inquiry:

(1) Does the believer *rely* upon these "texts" apart from *the use of his mind* or reason? This indicates passivity.
(2) Are these texts a prop to him (*a*) undermining his reliance on God Himself; (*b*) weakening his power of decision and his (proper) self-reliance?
(3) Do these texts influence him and (*a*) make him elated and puffed up as "specially guided by God," or (*b*) crush and condemn him, and throw him into despair and condemnation, instead of leading him to sober dealing with God Himself over the course of his life—with a keen and increasing knowledge of right and wrong obtained from the written Word by the light of the Holy Spirit?

If these and other such-like results are the fruit of the "texts" given, they may be rejected as from the deceiving spirits, or at least an attitude of neutrality should be taken concerning them until proof of their source is obtained.

The voice of the devil is also distinguishable from the voice of God by its purpose and outcome. If the outcome is not in accordance with the guidance given, then one definitely needs to check with fellow believers regarding its validity. For, obviously, if God speaks *directly* to a man, the man will then be infallibly correct with regard to the specific matter in question.

How Evil Spirits Adapt Their Guidance to Their Victim

Deceiving spirits carefully adapt their suggestions and leadings to the idiosyncrasies of the believer, so that they do not get found out; *i.e.*, no leading will be suggested contrary to any strong truth of God firmly rooted in the mind, or contrary to any special bias of the mind. If the mind has a practical bent, no visibly foolish leading will be given; if the Scriptures are well known, nothing contrary to Scripture will be said; if the believer feels strongly on any point, the leadings will be harmonized to suit that point. And, wherever possible, leadings will be adapted to previously true guidance from God so as to appear to be the continuance of that same guidance.

Here we see clearly the way of the enemy's working. The soul begins in God's will, but the purpose of the evil spirit is to draw it off into the carrying out of his will by counterfeiting the guidance of God. *Satanic* guidance alters the points of the life, and misdirects the energies of the man and lessens his service value. To frustrate this artifice of the enemy, the believer should know that there are two distinct attitudes with regard to guidance. There can be serious problems if their difference is not understood: *i.e.* (1) trusting *God* to guide, and (2) trust that God *is* guiding.

The first means *reliance upon God Himself*, and the second is an *assumption* of being guided which can be taken advantage of by deceiving spirits. In the first, God *does* guide in response to definite trust in Him, and He guides through the spirit of the man who continues to cooperate with His Spirit. Every faculty is left free to act, and one's will is able to choose intelligently the right step in the path before him.

In the second, when evil spirits take advantage of an assumption that God "is guiding" independent of momentary watchful cooperation with the Holy Spirit, a slight *compulsion* may be noticed, slowly increasing in force, until ultimately the believer says, "I was compelled" to do such-and-such, and "I was afraid to resist"—the compulsion being taken as an evidence of the guiding of God instead of recognized as being contrary to God's principle of dealing with His children.

The Deceived Believer a Slave to Evil Spirits

If false guidance is yielded to and believed to be of God, the result is that the believer becomes a slave to a supernatural power which destroys all freedom of volition and judgment. He begins to be afraid to act himself, lest he should not fulfill what he believes to be a minute obedience to the "will of God." He asks "permission" to do the most obviously simple duties of life, and fears to take a step without "permission." As soon as the believer is so passively automatic that he is incapable of realizing his condition, the evil spirits do not need to work so much under cover. They insidiously start directing him to do the most absurd or foolish things, carefully working inside the range of his passive obedience to their will so as to avoid the danger of awakening his reasoning powers. As a matter of "obedience," and not from any true conviction or true principle, he is bidden to let his hair grow long, so as to be like Samson, a Nazarite; to go without his cap, to prove his willingness to obey in the smallest matters; he must wear faded clothes as a "test" of "no pride" and a "crucifixion of self," or as a mark of "implicit obedience to God."

These things may seem trifles to others, who use their reasoning powers, but they become great issues in the purpose of the deceiving spirits, who, by these directions, aim at making the believer a passive, unthinking, or unreasoning medium, pliable to their will. By his obedience in these trivial matters, their hold deepens upon him.

When these foolish and absurd actions are publicly visible, the lying spirits know that they have destroyed the testimony of the deceived man in the eyes of sober people. But there are vast numbers of devoted believers—people known to the Church at large—who are not pushed to such "extremes" of exterior action but who are equally misled, or in bondage to "supernatural" commands concerning matters of food, dress, manner, etc., which they think they have received from God. Their spirit of judgment of others, and the secret self-esteem for their "consecration to God" which accompanies their "obedience," betrays the subtle workings of the enemy.

The "Planchette" Use of the Believer by Evil Spirits

As long as the believer thinks it is God who is directing him, so long the deceiving spirits are safe from exposure and able to lead him on into more and more deception. When the man reaches a very high degree of satanic deception he finds himself unable to act unless the spirits *allow him*, so that he no longer even asks for "permission" to do this or that.

At this stage, no arguments, reasonings, or outward considerations of any kind influence the actions of the believer thus deceived, or turn him from obeying the "guidance" or "permission" of the inner voice, which he fully believes is of God. Should he endeavor to go against it in the smallest matter, the condemnation and suffering are so great that he becomes terrified at any "disobedience," and would rather be condemned and misjudged by the whole world than go against it. His great horror is of "disobeying the Holy Ghost," and the evil spirits deceiving him take every occasion to deepen this fear, so as to retain their hold upon him.

As the believer thus minutely obeys the spirit in control, he relies more and more upon supernatural help, for the moment he does something apart from it he is accused—by the Holy Spirit, he assumes—of "working apart from God."

It is at this stage that all the faculties fall into deepening passivity, as the man lets go entirely to the voice of guidance—into a reliance upon the "divine" speakings, which keep his brain in complete inaction.

Here also counterfeit manifestations in "miraculous gifts"—prophecy, tongues, healings, visions, and supernatural experiences of every kind possible to the satanic powers—may be given to the believer, with abundant "texts" and "proofs" to confirm their "divine origin." He experiences a lightness of the body which makes it appear as if he were carried by invisible hands; he is lifted off his bed in what spiritists know as "levitation"; he can sing and speak, and do what he has never been capable of doing before. Constant contact with spirit forces gives the man a "mystical" look, but all lines of strength which come from strenuous conflict and self-mastery go out of the face, for the *sense-life* is being fed and indulged in a *spiritual* way as much as by fleshly habits.

The Counterfeiting of Human Traits

But counterfeits of God and divine things are not the only counterfeits the angel of light has at his command. Evil spirits can also counterfeit human personality traits. This falsifying may involve strangers, close acquaintances, and even the believer himself. Individuals will be made to appear different from what they really are—to be jealous, angry, critical or unkind. Self-centeredness is made to appear in others, in enlarged form, where there is really the very opposite tendency—selflessness and love. Wrong motives seem to govern acquaintances and friends; simple actions are colored, and words are made to mean and suggest what is not in the mind of the speaker—sometimes to the confirmation of supposed wrong-doings by that person.

Individuals of the opposite sex may also be *supernaturally portrayed* to a believer, in either a repulsive or beautiful form, with the object of arousing various dormant thoughts in the innocent believer which he or she does not realize exist within. Sometimes the reason for the inspection is masked as "for prayer," "for increased fellowship," or "for spirit-communion in the things of God."

When their influence is centered in the body, the lying spirits' counterfeit representation of these others may be in the realm of the passions and affections, seeking to rouse or feed these emotions in the oppressed one. The individual's face, voice, "presence," may be presented as if that person was equally affected. This is accompanied with a counterfeit "love" or drawing to the other one, with a painful craving for his or her company which almost masters the victim.

This subject of love, and its painful arousing and communicating or counterfeiting by evil spirits, is one that touches multitudes of believers of all classes. Many are made to suffer poignant agonies of craving for love, with no specific person involved; others are wrought upon in their thoughts so as not to be able to hear the word "love" mentioned without embarrassing manifestations of color*—none of these manifestations being under the control of the will of the believer.

THE COUNTERFEITING OF THE PERSON HIMSELF

In "counterfeiting" the believer himself, the evil spirit gives him exaggerated views, almost visions, of his own personality: he is "wonderfully gifted," and therefore becomes puffed up; he is "miserably incapable," and so is in despair; he is "amazingly clever," and thus undertakes what he cannot do; he is "helpless," "hopeless," "too forward" or "too backward"—in brief, a countless

* That is, *blushing*. In our day (1993), when nearly every newspaper, magazine, popular song and TV program is filled with sexual matters, how strange this sounds (Ed.).

number of false pictures of himself are presented to the mind of the man when once the lying spirit has gained a footing in his imagination.

Or this falsifying may take another form. So subtle is the identity of the deceiving spirit with a believer's individuality that only others will see what may be described as a "spurious personality." Sometimes the person appears to be "full of self" when the inner man is deeply selfless, "full of pride" when the inner man is sincerely humble. In fact, the whole outer appearance of the man in manner, voice, actions, words, is often quite contrary to his true character, and so he wonders why "others misunderstand," misjudge and criticize. Some believers, of course, will go on happily satisfied with what they themselves know of their own inner motives and heart life—oblivious of this manifestation of the spurious self which others behold, and pity or condemn.

The spurious personality caused by evil spirits can also be in a beautiful form, in order to attract or mislead others in various ways, all unwitting to the person or to the victim. This is sometimes described as "unaccountable infatuation," but if it was recognized as the work of evil spirits, refused and resisted, the "infatuation" would pass away. It is so wholly apart from the action of the will in the persons concerned that the work of evil spirits is clearly to be recognized, especially when the supposed "infatuation" follows supernatural experiences.

Counterfeit Sin

Evil spirits can also counterfeit sin, by causing some apparent manifestation of the evil nature in one's life. Mature believers should be able to tell whether such a manifestation really is sin from the old nature or a manifestation from evil spirits. The purpose in the latter case is to get the believer to take what comes from them as from himself, for whatever is accepted from evil spirits gives them power. When a believer knows the cross and his position of death to sin, and in his *will* and practice rejects unflinchingly all known sin, if a "manifestation" of personal sin takes place he should at once take a position of neutrality to it until he knows the source. If he calls it sin from himself when it is not, he believes a lie just as much as in any other way; and if he "confesses" as a sin what did not come from himself, he brings the power of the enemy upon him—power to drive him into the sin which he has confessed as his own. Many believers are thus held down by supposed "besetting sins" which they believe are theirs, and which no "confessing to God" removes, but from which they would find liberty if they attributed them to their right cause. There is no danger of "minimizing sin" in the recognition of these facts, because, in either case, the believer desires to be rid of the sins or he would not trouble himself about them.

COUNTERFEIT SELF-CONDEMNATION

Again, the believer is so acutely conscious of a "self" which he hates and loathes that he is never free from the dark shadow of self-condemnation, self-accusation or self-despair, which no appropriation of identification with Christ in death destroys; or else there is a self-confidence which continually draws the man forward into situations from which he has to retire abashed and disappointed. A spurious personality encompasses the true inner man—which few are aware is possible, but which is a sadly real thing among multitudes of the children of God.

On the part of the soul beset with these constant presentations to his mind of his own personality, he only thinks he has a "vivid imagination," or still more that some of these things are visions of God, and that he is favored of God, especially where the vision is of "great plans for God," or wide visions of what God is going to do! Always with the believer *himself* as the center and special instrument of this service!

Many of the plans for "great movements" (some of which have gone as far as into print) in connection with revivals have been of such a character—plans given by "revelation," and which have resulted in gaining but the few caught by them, and no others. Of such a character has been the aftermath of a revival where men have left their regular calling and followed a will-of-the-wisp revelation of "launching out on God"—world-wide plans conceived, and dissipated in a few months. Such deceived believers become ultra-devotional, with an excess of zeal that blinds them to all things but the supernatural realm, and robs them of power wisely to meet the claims of other aspects of life. All this comes from an evil spirit's access to the mind and imagination, through the deception of counterfeiting the presence of God.

COUNTERFEITS OF SATAN HIMSELF

Counterfeits of Satan himself also suit his purpose at times, when he desires to terrorize a man from actions, or prayer, adverse to his interests. Fear of the devil may always be regarded as *from* the devil, to enable him to carry out his plans of hindering the work of God. Of such a character may be the fearsome shrinking from hearing about him and his works, and the passive deadness of the mind in regard to all scriptural truth concerning the forces of evil. Also the fear caused by reference to his name, given in order to frighten away believers from knowing the facts about him. And others, who desire the truth, may be given exaggerated impressions of his presence, or of "conflict," "clouds," "blocks," "darkness," etc., until they lose the clearness of the light of God.

Especially is the work of the Deceiver manifested in

his efforts to make the children of God believe in his non-existence, and in the suggestion that it is only necessary to know about God for protection from the enemy's power. On the other hand, a deceived believer may be more deeply deceived by seeing nothing but Satan's counterfeits everywhere.

Supernatural visions and manifestations are a fruitful source of revenue to deceiving spirits, especially when the believer makes reference to and relies upon these experiences more than the Word of God; for the aim of the wicked spirit is to displace the Word of God as the rock-ground of one's life. Oh, the Scriptures may be referred to and quoted, but often only as a warrant for the experiences, and to strengthen faith—not in God, but in His apparent manifestations. This covert drawing of faith away from the bare Word of God to *manifestations* of God, as being more reliable, is a keenly subtle deception of the evil one, and it is easily recognized in a believer thus deceived.

COUNTERFEIT VISIONS

When evil spirits are able to give visions it is an evidence that they have already greatly deceived the man, be he a Christian or an unbeliever. The ground for this is not necessarily known sin, but a condition of passivity, *i.e.*, nonaction of the mind, imagination, and other faculties. This essential condition of submissive non-action as the means of obtaining supernatural manifestations is well understood by spiritist mediums, clairvoyants, crystal gazers, and others, who know that the least action of the mind immediately breaks the clairvoyant state.

Believers not knowing these basic principles can unwittingly fulfill the conditions for evil spirits to work in their life and ignorantly induce the passive state by wrong conceptions of the true things of God. For instance, they may (1) sink, during seasons of prayer, into a passive mental condition which they consider is "waiting on God"; (2) deliberately *will* the cessation of their mind action, in order to obtain some supernatural manifestations which they believe to be of God; (3) in daily life practice a passive attitude which they think is submission to the will of God; (4) endeavor to bring about a state of personal negation, in which they have no desires, needs, wishes, hopes, plans—which they think is full surrender to God, with their "will" lost in God.

Believers Can Ignorantly Develop Mediumistic Conditions

In brief, believers may unknowingly develop mediumistic conditions, of which deceiving spirits are not slow to take advantage. They are careful not to frighten the believer by doing anything which will open his eyes, so they keep within the range of what he will receive without question. They will portray the Lord Jesus in the particular way which will most appeal to the person, *e.g.*, to some as Bridegroom; to others as King on a throne, and coming in great glory. They will also impersonate the dead to those who grieve after their loved ones, and as they have watched them during life and know all about them, they will give ample "proofs" to confirm the deceived ones in their deception.

Visions may come from one of three sources: the divine, from God; the human, such as hallucinations and illusions because of disease; and the satanic, giving purposely false portrayals. Visions given by evil spirits can describe anything supernatural presented to and seen by the mind or imagination from outside, such as terrible pictures of the "future," the flashing of texts as if they were lit up, visions of wide-spreading "movements"—sometimes almost paralleling either a true vision of the Holy Spirit given to the "eye of the understanding" or a normal and healthy action of the imagination. The Church is thus often made a whirlpool of division through believers relying upon "texts" for guiding their decisions instead of depending on the principles of right and wrong set forth in God's Word.

The Detection of Visions as From God or Satan

Apart from the "visions" which are the result of disease, the detection of divine from satanic visions depends a great deal upon knowledge of the Word of God and the fundamental principles of His working in His children. These may be briefly stated thus:

(1) That no supernatural "vision," in any form, can be taken as of God if it requires a condition of *mental nonaction*, or comes while the believer is in such a condition.

(2) That all the Holy Spirit's enlightening and illuminating vision is given when the mind is in full use, and every faculty awake to understand; *i.e.*, the very opposite condition to that required for the working of evil spirits.

(3) That all which is of God is in harmony with the laws of God's working as set forth in the Scriptures, *e.g.*, "World-wide movements" by which multitudes are to be gathered in are not in accord with the laws of the growth of the Church of Christ, as shown in (*a*) the grain of wheat (John 12:24); (*b*) the law of the cross of Christ (Isa. 53:10); (*c*) the experience of Christ; (*d*) the experience of Paul (1 Cor. 4:9–13); (*e*) the "little flock" of Luke 12:32; (*f*) the foreshadowed end of the dispensation given in 1 Timothy 4:1–3 and 6:20–21.

Many a believer has left his path of "grain-of-wheat multiplication" caught by a vision of a "world-wide sweeping in" of souls—a concept given by Satan, whose malignant hatred and ceaseless antagonism is directed against the true *seed of Jesus Christ*, which in union with Him will bruise the serpent's head. To delay the birth (John 3:3,5) and growth of the holy seed (Isa. 6:13) is the devil's aim. To this end he will foster any widespread surface work of the believer, knowing it will not really touch his kingdom, nor hasten the full birth into the Throne-life of the conquering seed of Christ.

The safe path for believers at the close of the age is one of tenacious faith in the written Word as the sword of the Spirit, to cut the way through all the interferences and tactics of the forces of darkness, to the end.

Counterfeit Dreams

All dreams also, as well as visions, can be classed, as to their source, under three heads: (1) divine; (2) human; or (3) satanic—each to be known, first by the condition of the person, and second by the principles distinguishing the work of God or Satan.

The principle distinguishing divine from satanic in relation to dreams is, in the first instance, by their import and exceptional value (Gen. 37:5–7; Matt. 1:20, 2:12), and in the latter, their "mystery," absurdity, emptiness, folly, etc., as well as by their effects on the person. In the first, the recipient is left normal, calm, quiet, reasonable, and with an open, clear mind. In the second, elated or dazed, confused and unreasonable.

The presentations of evil spirits at night can be the cause of morning "dullness" of mind and heaviness of spirit. The sleep has not been refreshing because of their power, through the passivity of the mind during sleep, to influence the whole being. "Natural" sleep renews and invigorates the faculties and the whole system. Insomnia may be the work of evil spirits adapting their workings to the overwrought condition of the person, so as to keep their attacks under cover.

Believers who are open to the supernatural world should especially guard their nights by prayer, and by definite rejection of the first insidious workings of evil spirits along these lines.

How many say, "The Lord woke me," and place their reliance upon a "revelation" given in a state of half-consciousness, even though the mind and will were only partially alert to discern the issues of the "guidance" or "revelation" given to them. Let such believers observe the results of their obedience to night-revelations, however, and they will find many traces of the deceitful workings of the enemy. They will find, too, how their faith is often based upon a beautiful experience given in the early hours of the morning; or, vice versa, is shaken by accusations, suggestions, attacks and conflict manifestly of the evil one, instead of an intelligent reliance upon God Himself in His changeless character of faithfulness and love to His own.

All workings of the enemy at night can be made to cease by recognizing them as of him, and definitely refusing them in the name of the Lord.

CHAPTER 6

FREEDOM FOR THE DECEIVED

The very first step toward freedom is knowledge of the truth regarding the source and nature of experiences the believer may have had since his entrance into the spiritual life—experiences which possibly may have been perplexing, or else thought with deepest assurance to be of God. THERE IS NO DELIVERANCE FROM "DECEPTION" BUT BY THE ACKNOWLEDGMENT AND ACCEPTANCE OF TRUTH. And this *facing of truth* in regard to certain spiritual and "supernatural" experiences is like a keen-edged knife to a person's self-respect and pride.

THE HUMILIATION OF THE UNDECEIVING PERIOD

It requires a very deep allegiance to the truth which God desires should reign in the inward parts of His children for a believer to readily accept truth which cuts and humbles. The "undeceiving" is painful to the feelings. The discovery that he has been deceived is one of the keenest blows to a man who once thought that he was so "advanced," so "spiritual," and so "infallible" in his certainty of obeying the Spirit of God.

THE DISCOVERY OF THE TRUTH OF DECEPTION

The deceived believer laid claim to positions to which he had no right, for with the entrance of truth he discovers that he was neither so advanced, nor so spiritual, nor so infallible as he had thought. He built his faith about his own spiritual condition on assumption, and left no room for doubt—that is, true doubt, such as doubting a statement that afterwards turns out to be a lie. But in due season doubt finds an entry to his mind and brings his house of infallibility to the ground. He knows now that what he thought was an "advanced" experience was only a beginning, and that he is only on the fringe of knowledge. This is the operation of truth. In place of ignorance is given true knowledge; in place of deception, truth. Ignorance, falsehood and passivity—upon these three the enemy silently builds his castles, and unobtrusively guards and uses them. But truth pulls his strongholds to the ground.

By the entry of truth the man must be brought to the place where he acknowledges his condition frankly, as follows:

(1) I believe that it is POSSIBLE for a Christian to be deceived by evil spirits.
(2) It is possible for ME to be deceived.
(3) I AM deceived by an evil spirit.
(4) WHY am I deceived?

When the deception is of long standing, the spirits of evil may get the believer himself to defend their work in him, and *through him* fight tenaciously to guard the *cause* of his deception from being brought into light, and exposed as their work. They thus get the believer himself, in effect, to take their side, and fight *for them* to keep their hold, even after he has found out his condition and honestly desires deliverance.

THE SCRIPTURAL BASIS OF DELIVERANCE IN CALVARY'S VICTORY

The scriptural ground for obtaining deliverance is the truth concerning Christ's full victory at Calvary, through which every believer can be delivered from the power of both sin and Satan; but in actual fact the victory won at Calvary can only be applied as there is conformity to divine laws. As the deceptions of Satan are recognized, and the will of the Christian is set to reject them, he can, on the basis of the work of Christ at Calvary as set forth in Romans 6:6–13, Colossians 2:15, 1 John 3:8 and other passages, claim his deliverance from these workings of the devil in deception.

Just as there are various degrees of deception, so there are degrees of deliverance. These vary according to the understanding of the believer, and his *willingness to face all the truth about himself* and all the ground given to the enemy.

In doing this the believer needs to have a steady grasp of his standing in Christ: as identified with Him in His death on the cross, and his union with Him in spirit in His place on the Throne (Eph. 1:19–23; 2:6); and he must "hold fast," with steady faith-grip, the "Head" (Col. 2:19) as the One who is, by His Spirit, giving him grace (Heb. 4:16) and strength to recover the ground which he has ignorantly yielded to the foe. For the man himself must act to get rid of passivity; he must revoke his consent given to evil spirits to deceive, and by his own volition insist that they retire from the influence they have obtained by deceit (Eph. 4:27). Since God will not act for him in regaining the normal condition of his outer man, nor exercise his choice for him, he must stand on the vantage ground of the Calvary victory of Christ and claim his freedom.

Let us further examine the steps to freedom.

Doubt of the Experience

(1) *Doubt of the experience or "manifestation" being of God.* We cannot emphasize too strongly the need of not quenching and not ignoring the first doubt, for the "doubt" is actually the initial penetration of truth to the mind, and hence the first step to deliverance. Some have instantly quenched the first doubt, fearing to

"doubt God," and in doing so have closed their mind to the first ray of light which would have led them into liberty. They have looked upon doubt as temptation, and resisted it, overlooking the distinction between true and evil, right and wrong "doubt." This has its root in the mind of most Christians in associating only *evil* with such words as "judging," "criticizing," "doubting," and "enmity," "hatred," "unbelief," etc.—all of which dispositions and actions they thought to be evil, and evil only, whereas they are evil or *good* according to their *source* in spirit or soul, and in relation to their object. For example, "enmity" against Satan is God-given (Gen. 3:15), "hatred" toward sin is good, and "unbelief" of spirit manifestations is commanded until the believer is sure of their source (1 John 4:1).

To doubt God—which means not to trust Him—is sin; but a doubt concerning supernatural manifestations is simply a call to exercise the faculties which all spiritual believers should use to discern "good and evil." The deep doubt concerning some supernatural experiences is therefore not a "temptation" but is really the Holy Spirit moving the spiritual faculties to action according to 1 Corinthians 2:15: *"He that is spiritual judgeth—i.e.,* examineth—*all things,"* the "things of God" thus being "spiritually discerned" (v. 14, KJV).

No Contradiction in the Working of the Spirit of God

A doubt generally first pierces the mind either from truth pointed out by others, or arises from some flaw in the experience which arrests the attention of the believer. In the case of some supernatural manifestation, for instance, which bore the appearance of being divine, there was some slight contradiction which perplexed the soul. And as no contradictions can possibly occur in any of the workings of the Spirit of God, who is the Spirit of Truth, *one single contradiction* is sufficient to reveal a lying spirit at work. *This axiom must not be ignored.* For instance, a believer declares under supernatural "power"—assumed to be divine—concerning one who is ill, that God purposes the restoration of that one, yet the sick one dies. This is a "contradiction" which should be fully examined, and not put aside as among things "not to be understood"; for the supernatural element in the declaration could not be of the Spirit of God, who cannot depart from truth in His revelation of the will of God.

To "prove the spirits" (1 John 4:1), so as to discern between the "Spirit of Truth" and the "spirit of error," is a clear command to the children of God, as well as to "prove all things" and "hold fast that which is good" (1 Thess. 5:21); bring "to the proof . . . with all longsuffering" (2 Tim. 4:2, mg.). To question until all things have stood the test of full examination is the safest course, and is far removed from the doubting of God Himself, in His faithfulness and love—the only doubt which is sin.

Admittance of Possibility of Deception

(2) *Admittance of the possibility of deception* is the second stage in the breaking of truth upon the mind, although it may sometimes precede the doubt. To admit the *possibility* of being deceived—or mistaken—in any aspect of new experience or action, or even view of truth, is really a possibility which should be acknowledged by every believer; and yet so subtle is the deception of the enemy that almost invariably the attitude of each one is that though "others" may be open to deception, he or she is the exception to the rule.

This certainty of personal exception is so deep-seated with the most visibly deceived person that the longest battle is simply to obtain entrance to the mind for the one thought of possible deception in any point at all. The believer seems armed with unshaken assurance that though others may be misled, he certainly is not; he "beholdeth the mote" in his brother's eye and is blind—blind to the "beam" in his own. But an open attitude to truth says, "*Why not I as well as others?* May not my assurance of safety be a deception of the enemy, as much as the deception I see in others?"

Why *all* believers should admit the possibility of deception by deceiving spirits may be considered just here:

The Basic Fact of the Fall

The primary fact to be recognized by every human being is the complete and utter ruin of the first creation at the Fall—when the first Adam admitted the poison of the serpent, which permeated and corrupted his whole being beyond repair. The utter corruption of the human race as a consequence is unmistakably declared in the New Testament:

"The old man, which waxeth corrupt after the lusts of deceit" (Eph. 4:22).

"Being darkened in their understanding; alienated from the life of God" (Eph. 4:18).

"*We all once lived* in the lusts of the flesh, doing the desires of the flesh and of the thoughts, and were by nature the children of wrath, even as the rest" (Eph. 2:3, mg.).

Thus the Apostle Paul described the whole race of man, Gentile and Jew, Pharisee and Publican: In all, he said, "the prince of the power of the air" has operated, as "the spirit that now worketh in the sons of disobedience."

Admittance of Possible Deception Logically Reasonable

The second fundamental fact—and the logical outcome of the first—is that unless regeneration by the Holy Spirit and the indwelling of the Spirit means (1) sinlessness, and (2) the present possession of a resurrection body, *not every part of a believer is yet renewed* and freed by the redemption of Calvary from the effects of the Fall. HENCE THERE IS GROUND FOR THE POSSIBLE OPERATION OF DECEIVING SPIRITS. Since absolute sinlessness and the present possession of the resurrection body are not taught in the Scriptures as attainable while on earth, the chance of deception is logically and reasonably possible—even while the spirit and heart of the man is renewed by the Holy Spirit. If we come to facts of experience, the proofs are so abundant as to be beyond our capacity to handle in the limited space of this book, not only in the unregenerate world but in those who are undoubtedly children of God and spiritual believers.

If we knew ourselves and our actual condition as sinners, as depicted in God's Word, we would be in greater safety from the enemy. It is the ignorance of our true condition even with the new life from God implanted in us, and our blind confidence of safety without an intelligent basis for that assumption, which lays us open to being deceived by Satan through our very certainty of being free from his deception.

THE DISCOVERY AND ACKNOWLEDGMENT OF DECEPTION

After admitting the possibility of deception in supernatural things, and a doubt has come into the mind whether certain "experiences," either personal or otherwise, were of God after all, the next stages are:

(3) *The discovery of the deception.* Light and truth alone can make free, and when once a doubt comes in and the man opens his mind to the truth that he is as liable to be deceived as anyone else, then to the open mind and attitude light is given (John 3:21). Sometimes the specific deception is seen at once, but more often the discovery is gradual, and patience is needed

while the light slowly dawns.

Certain facts in connection with various experiences of the past, which the believer has failed to note, may now emerge into the light, and the half-truths which the Adversary had used to deceive are clearly seen: the twisting of words, the wrenching of sentences out of their context in the Scriptures—all come into view as the light is given. Then comes:

(4) *The acknowledgment of the deception.* This is now imperative. The truth must not only be faced but *owned up to*, so that things are called by their right names, and the father of lies defeated by the weapon of truth.

THE TACTICS OF THE ENEMY DURING THE FIGHTING-THROUGH PERIOD

When the spirits of evil see their hold coming to an end, they never let go until the cause is fully removed. They continue to attack if the thing they have attacked about still exists in any degree. When the Christian is "fighting through," the enemy has various tactics to hinder his deliverance. He may dangle a thing before the mind which is not the true cause of the deception, so as to get the believer occupied with it, while he is gaining all the time—pouring in accusations upon his victim until he is bewildered and confused: charges, accusations, blame, guilt—direct from the enemy, or indirectly through others. Accusing spirits can say "You are wrong" when you are not wrong, and vice versa; and also say you are wrong when you *are* wrong, and right when you *are* right—but it is essential that the believer does not accept blame until he is absolutely sure that it is deserved, and then not from Satan's lying spirits; they have not been appointed by God to do the convicting work of the Holy Spirit.

When once the truth has dawned upon the victim of the powers of darkness, and they no longer hope to gain by deception, their one primary attack all through—from the moment of undeceiving to final deliverance—is the perpetual charge "You are wrong," so as to keep the man in ceaseless condemnation. The poor persecuted believer then is likely to go to God and try to get victory over "sin," but in vain. The more he prays, the more he appears to sink into a hopeless bog. He seems to himself to be one mass of "sin," without hope of freedom. But it is victory over *the powers of darkness*—not *sin*—that he needs, and he will quickly prove this when he recognizes the true cause of his trouble and lays hold of the Calvary victory over Satan.

The Weapon of Scripture

In fighting back to freedom, the believer must wield Scripture as the divinely provided weapon for victory over evil spirits. The verses used with immediate effect, and giving evidence of relief, indicate the specific nature of any attack. They show by the efficacy of the weapon used the immediate cause of the conflict—as the believer reasons back from the effectiveness of the weapon to the cause of the warfare. For instance, if the text wielded is that Satan is the "father of lies," and the believer declares that he refuses all his lies, and this brings liberty from the oppression of the enemy, it indicates that the enemy is attacking with some of his deceptive workings. Then the believer should not only refuse all his lies, but pray, *"Lord, destroy all the devil's lies to me."*

All this simply means is that in the path to freedom the deceived believer must act intelligently. He must *know the truth*, and when the truth is received and acted upon he is set free. In going down into deception the intelligence is *unused*, but in recovering freedom he must act with deliberate knowledge; *i.e.*, he goes down "passively," but he must emerge to liberty actively, by the action of his whole being.

Force must be used against force. The deceiving

spirits may suggest that this is "self-effort," and attempt to again deceive the man into taking a passive attitude—so beware!

A few brief suggestions for attitude and action may be added here in condensed form, for the guidance of any who are seeking freedom from the enemy's power:

(1) Keep claiming the power of the blood (Rev. 12:11).
(2) Pray for light, and face the past.
(3) Resist the devil persistently in your spirit.
(4) Never give up hope.
(5) Avoid all introspection.
(6) Live and pray for others, and thus keep your spirit in full aggressive and resisting power.

Again it may be said:

(1) Stand daily on Romans 6:11 as the *attitude* to sin.
(2) Resist the enemy (James 4:7) daily on the ground of the blood of Christ (Rev. 12:11).
(3) Live daily for others; live outward, and not inward.

STANDING ON ROMANS 6:11, A WEAPON OF VICTORY

"Stand daily on Romans 6:11"—what does this mean? It has reference to the attitude of the believer: reckoning himself "dead unto sin . . . in Christ Jesus." It is a declaration of death—a gulf of death—to evil spirits as well as sin.

To resist the enemy on the ground of the blood of Christ means wielding the weapon of the finished work of Christ, by faith: believing that Jesus' death for sin frees the trusting believer from the *guilt* of sin; that Jesus' death to sin on the cross, and the believer's death with Him, frees the Christian from the *power* of sin; and that Jesus' death-victory on Calvary frees the believer also from the power of *Satan.*

A condensed form of the principles and conditions for deliverance from the deception of evil spirits in any degree may be given as follows:

(1) Recognition of the possibility of deception.
(2) Admission of actual deception.
(3) An attitude of neutrality toward all past spiritual experiences until truth concerning them is ascertained.
(4) Refusal of all ground to evil spirits.
(5) The taking of the position of death to sin (Rom. 6:11).
(6) The detection and refusal of all that belongs to deception.
(7) The understanding of the criterion of the true, normal condition so as to gauge signs of deliverance.
(8) Active usage of the faculties so that they reach the normal condition.

In another, briefer form, a summary of the steps to deliverance may be given as follows:

(1) Recognize persistently the true cause of bondage; *i.e.*, the work of an evil spirit or spirits.
(2) Choose to have absolutely nothing to do with the powers of darkness. Frequently declare this.
(3) Do not talk or worry about their manifestations. Recognize, refuse, and *then ignore them.*
(4) Refuse and reject all their lies and excuses, as they are recognized.
(5) Notice the thoughts, and the way in which they come, and when—and immediately declare the attitude of Romans 6:11 against all the interferences of the enemy.

Hindrances to deliverance from deception may again be given here briefly, as:

(1) Not knowing it is possible to be deceived.
(2) Thinking God will not allow a believer to be deceived.
(3) Saying "I am safe under the blood," without intelligent knowledge of the conditions.
(4) Saying "I have no sin."
(5) Saying "I am doing all that God wants, so all must be right"—without seeking to *understand* what the will of the Lord is (Eph. 5:10–17).

Some hints on overcoming passivity of mind are as follows:

(1) Act as far as you can, doing what you can.
(2) Take the initiative, instead of passively depending on others.
(3) Decide for yourself in everything you can. Do not lean on others.
(4) Live in the moment; watch and pray step by step.
(5) Use your mind, and *think*—think over all you do, and say, and are.

Naming the Attack a Factor in Victory

Naming the "attack" is a great factor for victory. For example, an attack may be made to hinder; then the believer must be on guard against all hindrances, seen and unseen, which the hinderer is placing in his way. Or it may be to make him impatient; then he must be on guard regarding all things liable to test his patience. The sooner the attack is recognized and named, the quicker the weapon can be called into use to destroy it.

It may be a flood of accusations of wrongdoing which need to be recognized, or tested as to their truth. When the accusing spirit charges a person with some specific wrong over a certain thing, and the believer surrenders that thing to God, if the accusation does not then pass away it shows that it is not the true ground for the accusation, but there is some other cause hidden from view. The believer should then seek light from God upon the hidden causes, according to John 3:21, and *refuse* the cause of the accusation without knowing what it is, saying, "I refuse the cause of this attack, whatever it is, and I trust the Lord to destroy it."

The Importance of Knowing One's Normal Condition

It is essential, and indispensable for full deliverance from deception by evil spirits, that a believer knows the standard of his normal condition, for with this gauge before him he can judge his degree of deliverance—physically, intellectually and spiritually—so as to fight through with steady volition and faith until every faculty is free, and he stands as an unshackled man in the liberty wherewith Christ has made him free.

As he judges himself by this criterion he may say, "Things are not the same as they were"; so he then fights through by prayer to his normal condition. The deceiving spirits will suggest all kinds of excuses to stop the man's advance to freedom; *e.g.*, if he is forty years of age, they will suggest that "the mind cannot be as vigorous as it was at twenty"; or "overwork is the cause of your being below what you should be." But he must not accept reasons which appear to be "natural."

Some practical ways of keeping the mind in its normal working condition may be briefly suggested as follows:

(1) One's attitude toward the past. There should be no regrets, or brooding over things done or undone. Evaluation is an ordinary operation of the mind when thinking over the past, but it can be entangled into an evil kind of thinking which is generally described as "brooding." The believer must learn to discern for himself if he is simply "thinking" or is being drawn into a state of regretting or brooding.

For victory in one's life there must be victory in regard to the past, with all its failures. The *good* events of the past cause no trouble to the mind, only those involving real or supposed *evil*. They should be dealt with by coming to God on the ground of 1 John 1:9, and thus the believer will be delivered.

(2) ONE'S ATTITUDE TOWARD THE FUTURE. The same may be said about the action of the mind with regard to the future. It is lawful to *think* of the past and *think* of the future, so long as the evil state of "brooding," brought about by sin, or Satan, is not yielded to.

(3) ONE'S ATTITUDE TOWARD EVIL SPIRITS. They must not be permitted to interfere; the believer should see to it that no new ground is given to them for deception.

(4) ONE'S ATTITUDE TOWARD THE PRESENT MOMENT. There should be a steady concentration of mind upon the duties of the moment, keeping it in active readiness for use as occasion requires. This does not mean ceaseless activity, of course. Activity of the mind so that it is never at rest can be a symptom of deception.

THE WEAPON OF THE WORD OF GOD

The believer must understand that the regaining of the facile use of his faculties, and the maintenance of his mind in healthy condition after recovery from passive surrender to evil spirits, will mean a steady fight with the powers of darkness—requiring the use of the weapons of warfare given in the Word of God. Weapons, for instance, such as the truth in the text "Sufficient for the day is the evil thereof," for resisting brooding over the past, or torturing pictures of the future; "Resist the devil and he will flee from you," when the pressure of the enemy is severe; and other "fighting" texts, which will prove truly to be the "sword of the

Spirit" to thrust at the enemy in the "evil day" of his onslaught upon the escaping believer.

(5) THE STEADY ATTITUDE OR ACTION OF ONE'S WILL. In keeping the mind in normal working condition, free from the interference of the enemy, the believer should maintain the attitude of having his will steadily set: *i.e.*, "I *will* that my mind shall not be passive"; "I *will* to have full control of my faculties, and to use them"; "I *will* to recognize everything that comes from the enemy"—each of which declares the CHOICE of the man, rather than his *determination* to do these things. The powers of darkness are not affected by mere determination—*i.e.*, resolve—but they are rendered powerless by the act of the will definitely *choosing*, in the strength given by God, to stand against them.

These steps to deliverance which have been given deal with THE PRACTICAL ASPECT OF THE BELIEVER'S ACTIONS. On the divine side, the victory *has been won*, and Satan and his deceiving spirits *have been conquered;* but the actual liberation of the believer demands his *active cooperation with the Holy Spirit*, plus the steady exercise of his volition—choosing freedom instead of bondage. This will result in the normal use of every faculty of his being, set at liberty from the bondage of the enemy.

"He that doeth the truth cometh to the light," said the Lord (John 3:21). Evil spirits hate scrutiny, and so work under cover with deception and lies. The believer must come to the light of God for His light upon all spiritual experiences (as well as in all other departments of life) if he is to "cast off the works of darkness" (Rom. 13:12) and put on the armor of God—the armor of light.

CHAPTER 7

Volition and the Human Spirit

It is now necessary to see from the Scriptures the true way in which God works in the believer, for the principle of cooperation with God rather than passive control by Him must be fully understood.

Briefly, it may be said that the Holy Spirit dwelling in the regenerate human spirit energizes and works through the faculties of the soul and the members of the body only in and with the active cooperation of the WILL of the believer. In other words, God, though in the spirit of the man, does not use the man's hand apart from the "I will use my hand" of the man himself.

Cooperation With God Does Not Mean Automatic Working

When Paul, in Colossians 1:29, spoke of "His working, which worketh in me mightily," he first said, "I labor according to His working." Did the "I labor" mean that his hands and feet and mind worked automatically in response to a divine energizing, as an engine works in response to the steam? No. At the back of the "I labor" was the full action of Paul's will, saying "I choose to labor," and "as I labor, God's power and energy energizes me in the acting," so that it is "I who live and move and work," and "yet not I, but Christ—the 'Spirit of Christ'—in me" (see Gal. 2:20; Phil. 1:19).

It was so in the Greater-than-Paul, who said, "I came not to do Mine own will, but the will of Him that sent

Me," and "The Son can do nothing of Himself." And yet He said also, "My Father worketh hitherto and *I work*" and "The works that *I do* shall ye do also"! He had a separate will, but He came not to do His own will but the will of the Father, and He was doing the Father's will when He said to the one who sought His healing power, "*I will*, be thou clean."

Thus it should be in the life of the believer. Granted the essential union of his will with the will of God, and the energizing power of the Holy Spirit, by his own deliberate choice of harmony with that holy will the believer is actively to use his will in ruling himself in spirit, soul and body. God dwelling in his spirit cooperates with him through his exercised power of choice.

God Governs the Renewed Man by His Co-acting Will

For deliverance from the power of sin and protection from deceiving spirits in their workings, it is important to have a clear understanding of God's purpose in redemption. God created man with dominion over himself. This dominion was to be exercised by Adam's acts of will, even as it was by his Creator. But man fell, and in his fall he yielded his will to the rule of Satan who, from that time, by the agency of his evil spirits, has ruled the world through the enslaved will of fallen man. Christ, the Second Adam, came, and, taking the place of man, chose obedience to the Father's will, and never for one moment diverged from His perfect cooperation with that will. In the wilderness He refused to exercise His divine power at the will of Satan, and even while suffering in Gethsemane His will never wavered in the choice of the Father's will. As man He willed the will of God right through, becoming obedient even unto death, thus regaining for regenerated man not only reconciliation with God but liberty from Satan's thralldom, and the restoration of man's renewed and sanctified will to its place of free action, deliberately and intelligently exercised in harmony with the will of God.

Christ worked out for man upon Calvary's cross salvation of spirit, soul and body from the dominion of sin and Satan; but that full salvation is worked out in the believer through the central action of the will, as he deliberately chooses the will of God for each department of his tripartite nature.

The will of the man united to the will of God—and thus having the energizing power of God working with his volition*—is to rule his (1) "*own spirit*" (see Prov. 25:28; 1 Cor. 14:32); (2) *thoughts or mind* (Col. 3:2) inclusive of all the soul-powers; and (3) *body* (1 Cor. 9:27). And when, by the appropriation of God's freeing power from slavery to sin and Satan, the believer regains free action of his will so that he gladly and spontaneously wills the will of God, and as a renewed man retakes dominion over spirit, soul and body, he reigns in life "through . . . Jesus Christ" (Rom. 5:17).

But the natural man does not reach this stage of renewal and liberation of his will without first knowing the regeneration of his own human spirit. God is not in fallen man until the moment of his *new birth* (Eph. 2:12; 3:16; John 3:5–8). He must be "begotten of God." The very fact of such a begetting being necessary declares the non-existence of divine life in him previously. It is essential to understand, however, that after this begetting the regenerated man does not, as a rule, immediately become a spiritual man, *i.e.*, a man wholly dominated by and walking after the spirit.

THE "NATURAL" VERSUS THE "SPIRITUAL" MAN

At first the regenerated man is but a "babe in Christ," manifesting many of the characteristics of the natural

---

* That is, his power of choice, or his willing consent (Ed.).

man in jealousy, strife, etc., until he apprehends the need of a fuller reception of the Holy Spirit to dwell in his regenerated spirit—making it God's sanctuary.

The unregenerate man is wholly dominated by soul and body. The regenerate man has his spirit (1) quickened, and (2) indwelt by the Holy Spirit, yet may be governed by soul and body because his spirit is compressed and bound. The spiritual man has his spirit liberated from bondage to the soul (Heb. 4:12) to be the organ of the Holy Spirit in mind and body.

It is then that, by the Holy Spirit's power, his volition is brought into harmony with God in all His laws and purposes, and the whole outer man into self-control. Thus it is written, "The fruit of the Spirit . . . is self-control" (Gal. 5:23, mg.). It is not only love, joy, peace, longsuffering and gentleness, manifested through the channel of the soul—the personality—but in a true dominion over the "world" of himself the fruit is: (1) every thought brought into captivity, in the same obedience to the will of the Father as was manifested in Christ (2 Cor. 10:5); (2) his spirit "ruled" also from the chamber of the will, so that he is of a "cool spirit" and can keep back or utter at his will what is in his spirit as well as what is in his mind (Prov. 17:27); and (3) his body so obedient to the helm of the will that it is a disciplined and alert instrument for God to energize and empower—an instrument to be handled intelligently as a vehicle for service, and not any longer master of the man, or the mere tool of Satan and unruly desires.

THE CALL TO DECISIVE ACTION OF THE WILL

All this is made fully clear in the New Testament Epistles. "Our old man was crucified with Him" is said of us in light of the work of Christ at Calvary; but the believer who desires this fact made personally true in his life is called upon to declare his attitude of choice with decisive action, both in the negative and positive positions. The apostle appeals again and again to the redeemed believer to act decisively with his will, as the following few passages show:

Negative	Positive
"Cast off the works of darkness." Rom. 13:12.	"Put on the armor of light." Rom. 13:12.
"Put away the old man." Eph. 4:22.	"Put on the new man." Eph. 4:24.
"Put off the old man with his doings." Col. 3:9.	"Put on the new man." Col. 3:10.
"Put to death your members." Col. 3:5.	"Present your members unto God." Rom. 6:13.
"Put off the body of the flesh." Col. 2:11.	"Put on the Lord Jesus and make no provision for the flesh." Rom. 13:14.

See also:

"Take up the whole armor . . ."	Eph. 6:15–16.
"Put on a heart of compassion."	Col. 3:12.
"Put on the whole armor of God."	Eph. 6:11.

All these passages describe a decisive act of the will, not toward exterior things but toward things in an unseen, immaterial sphere. They incidentally show the effect in the spiritual sphere of a man's volitional action. They also emphasize the effect of the decisive use of the will of man—*when it acts in harmony with the liberating power of Christ.* Christ has done the work on Calvary's cross, but that work is applied in fact through the action of the believer's own will, acting as if he himself had power to "cast off" the invisible works of darkness. He finds with this action of his will the coworking of the Spirit of God—making the casting off effectual.

In saving the man, God calls him into co-action with Himself, to "work out his own salvation," for it is the Holy Spirit who works with and in him, to enable him to will and to do God's pleasure (Phil. 2:12–15).

God Calls a Man Into Co-action for His Own Salvation

God gives to the man in the hour of his regeneration the decisive liberty of will to rule over himself, as he walks in fellowship with God. And by this restoration of a will free to act in choosing for God, *Satan loses his power.* Satan is the god of this world, and he rules the world through the will of men enslaved by him—enslaved not only directly but indirectly, by his inciting men to enslave one another and to covet the power of "influence," whereas they should work with God to restore to every man the freedom of his own personal volition, and the power of choice to *do* right because it *is* right—the power obtained for them at Calvary.

In this direction we can see the working of the world-rulers of darkness in the realm which they govern, directly in atmospheric influence and indirectly through men, in (1) hypnotic suggestions, (2) mind reading, (3) manipulation of the will, and other forms of invisible force, sometimes employed for the supposed good of others.

The danger of all forms of healing by "suggestion," and all kindred methods of seeking to benefit men in physical or mental ways, lies in their bringing about a *passivity of the will* and *mental powers* which lays them open to satanic influences later on.

The Believer's Right of Decision of Will

The liberation of the will from its passive condition and control by the prince of this world takes place when the believer recognizes his right of choice and begins deliberately to place his will on God's side, thus choosing the will of God. Until the will is fully liberated for action, it is helpful for the believer to assert his decision frequently by saying, "I choose the will of God, and I refuse the will of Satan." The soul may not even be able to distinguish which is which, but the declaration is having effect in the unseen world. God definitely works by His Spirit in the man as he chooses His will, energizing him through his volition continually to refuse the claims of sin and Satan; and Satan is thereby rendered more and more powerless, while the man is stepping out into the salvation obtained potentially for him at Calvary . . . and God is gaining once more a loyal subject in a rebellious world.

On the part of the believer the action of the will is governed by the understanding of the mind: *i.e.*, the mind sees what to do, the will chooses to do it, and then from the spirit comes the power to fulfill the choice of the will and the percept of the mind. For example, the man (1) sees that he should speak, (2) he chooses or wills to speak, (3) he draws upon the power in his spirit to carry out his decision. This presumes a knowledge of how to use the spirit and involves the necessity of knowing the laws of the spirit, so as to cooperate fully with the Holy Ghost.

THE SPIRIT ENERGIZED BY THE HOLY SPIRIT AT THE BACK OF THE WILL

But the believer thus cooperating with God in the use of his volition must understand that the choice of the will is not sufficient alone, as we see by Paul's words in Romans 7:18: "To will is present with me, but to *do* . . . is not." Through the spirit, and by the strengthening of the Holy Spirit in the "inward man" (the regenerate human spirit*—Eph. 3:16), is the liberated will—desiring and determined to do God's will—empowered to carry out its choice. "It is *God* which worketh in you . . . to will," *i.e.*, to enable the believer to decide or choose. Then it is "God which worketh in

---

* Bishop Moule.

you . . . to *do* His good pleasure" (Phil. 2:13, KJV), *i.e.*, He energizes the believer with power to carry out the choice.

In short, God gives the power to do—acting from the spirit where He dwells. But the believer needs to understand the use of his spirit as clearly as he understands the use (1) of his will, (2) of his mind, or (3) of his body. He must know how to discern the sense of his spirit so as to understand the will of God, before he can do it.

THE DISTINCT ORGANISM OF THE SPIRIT

That the human spirit is a distinct organism, separate from the soul and body, is very clearly recognized in the Scriptures—as these few verses show:

"The spirit of man." ______________ 1 Cor. 2:11.
"My spirit prayeth." ______________ 1 Cor. 14:14.
"The Spirit Himself beareth witness with our spirit." __________ Rom. 8:16.
". . . my spirit . . ." ______________ 1 Cor. 5:4.
"Relief in my spirit." ______________ 2 Cor. 2:13.*

There is also a "separation of soul and spirit" required and carried out by the Word of God—the sword of the Spirit; so we are informed in Hebrews 4:12. This is because of the Fall. The spirit which had been in union with God—which once ruled and dominated the soul and body—fell from it's predominant position into the vessel of the soul† and could no longer rule. In the "new birth," which the Lord told Nicodemus was necessary for every man, the regeneration of the fallen spirit takes place. "That which is born of the Spirit is spirit" (John 3:6); "a *new spirit* will I put within you"

* See also Psalm 77:3, 6; Dan. 7:15; Ezek. 3:14; Ezek. 11:19; Rom. 7:6; Acts 19:21; 2 Cor. 7:13; 1 Cor. 6:18.
† Faussett.

(Ezek. 36:26). And through cognizance of the death of the old creation with Christ, as set forth in Romans 6:6, is the new spirit liberated, divided from the soul, and joined to the Risen Lord. "Dead to the law . . . joined to Another"; "Having died . . . that we might serve in newness of the spirit" (Rom. 7:4–6).

The believer's life is therefore to be a walk "after the spirit," minding "the things of the spirit" (Rom. 8:4–5). In the Revised Version (of 1881), at these verses, the word "spirit" is not written with a capital "S," denoting the Spirit of God, but with a small "s," referring to the spirit of man.* But the believer can only thus walk "after the spirit" if the Spirit of God dwells in him (Rom. 8:9). The Holy Spirit lifts one's spirit to the place of rule over soul and body—"flesh," both ethically and physically—by joining it to the Risen Lord, and making it "one spirit" with Him (1 Cor. 6:17).

That the believer retains volitional control over his own spirit is the important point to note, for through ignorance he can withdraw his spirit from cooperation with the Holy Spirit, and thus, so to speak, "walk after the soul," or "after the flesh"—unwittingly. A surrendered will to do the will of God is therefore no guarantee that he is doing that will; he must understand what the will of the Lord is (Eph. 5:17), and for the doing of that will must seek to be filled in spirit to the utmost of his capacity.

The knowledge that the Spirit of God has come to indwell the shrine of the spirit is not enough to guarantee that the believer will continue to walk in the spirit and not fulfill the lusts of the flesh (Gal. 5:16). If he wishes to truly "live" in the realm of the Spirit and know His power, he must learn how to "walk" with the Spirit. And for this, he must understand how to "combine"

* See also The New Berkeley Version and Weymouth's New Testament in Modern Speech (Ed.).

and "compare" spiritual things with spiritual (1 Cor. 2:13, RV and KJV), so as to interpret truly the things of the Spirit of God—exercising the spirit faculty by which he is able to examine all things, and so discern the mind of the Lord.

Such a believer should know how to walk after the spirit, so that he does not quench its action, movements or admonitions as it is moved or exercised by the Spirit of God—cultivating its strength by use, so that he becomes "strong in spirit" (Luke 1:80), and a truly spiritual man of "full age" in the Church of God (1 Cor. 2:6; Heb. 6:1).

How Believers Ignore the Human Spirit

Many believers are not even aware that they have a spirit. At the other extreme, however, some people imagine that every experience which takes place in the realm of their senses is spirit-based—or perhaps even directly "of the Spirit." These believers consider everything which takes place in their inner life to be His working.

In each of these cases the man's own spirit is left out of account. In the first instance, the believer's religious life is, if we may say so, "spiritually mental," that is, the *mind* is illuminated and enjoys spiritual truth, but what "spirit" means he does not clearly know. In the second instance the believer is really "soulish," although he thinks he is spiritual. And in the case where the believer thinks that the Holy Spirit's indwelling means every movement is of Him, he becomes dangerously open to the deception of evil spirits counterfeiting the Holy Spirit, because without discrimination he attributes all inner "movements" or experiences to Him.

The Human Spirit Co-working With the Holy Spirit

Walking "after the spirit" and "minding the spirit"—

these expressions do not merely mean mind and body are subservient to the spirit, but they denote the man's own spirit co-working with the Holy Spirit in his daily life, and in all the occasions of life. To do this, the believer needs to know the laws of the spirit—not only the conditions necessary for the Holy Spirit's working but the laws also governing his own spirit, so that it may be kept open to the Spirit of God.

When the Holy Spirit takes the spirit of man as His sanctuary, evil spirits attack the spirit to get it out of co-working with God. They seek to deceive the mind, their object being to close the outlet of the Spirit of God dwelling at the center. And yet, when the man is "spiritual" and the mind and body is subservient to the spirit, the spiritual forces of Satan can come into DIRECT CONTACT with the spirit—and then follows the "wrestling" referred to by Paul (Eph. 6:12).

If the man is ignorant of the laws of the spirit, especially the tactics of Satan, he is liable to yield to an onslaught of deceiving spirits by which they (1) force his spirit into strained ecstasy, or elation, or else (2) press it down, as it were, into a vice. In the former case he is given "visions" and revelations which appear to be divine, but afterwards are proved to have been of the enemy, by their passing away with no results; in the latter, the man sinks into darkness and deadness as if he had lost all knowledge of God.

THE BELIEVER'S CONTROL OVER HIS SPIRIT

When the believer understands these direct onslaughts of wicked spirits, he becomes able to discern the condition of his spirit and to retain control over it—refusing all forced elation and strain and resisting all weights and pressure to drive it below the normal state of poise—so that it is capable of cooperation with the Spirit of God.

The danger of the human spirit acting out of cooperation with the Holy Spirit and becoming driven or influenced by deceiving spirits is a very serious one, yet it can be increasingly detected by those who walk softly and humbly with God. For instance, a man is liable to think his own masterful spirit is an evidence of the power of God because in other directions he sees the Holy Spirit using him in winning souls. In another instance, one may have a flood of indignation inserted into his spirit which he pours out thinking it is all of God, though others shrink and are conscious of a harsh note which is clearly not of God.

This influence on the human spirit by evil spirits counterfeiting the divine workings—or even the workings of the man himself, because he is out of co-working with the Holy Spirit—needs to be understood and detected by the believer who seeks to walk with God. He needs to know that because he is spiritual his spirit is open to two forces of the spirit-realm, and that if he thinks only the Holy Spirit can influence him in the spiritual sphere he is likely to be misled. If such were so, he would become infallible; but he needs to watch and pray, and seek to have the eyes of his understanding enlightened to know the true workings of God.

Some Laws Governing the True Spirit Life

Some of the laws governing the spirit life may be summarized briefly as follows:

(1) The believer must know what is spirit, and how to give heed to the demands of the spirit and not quench it: *e.g.*, a weight comes on his spirit, but he goes on with his work, putting up with the pressure; he finds the work hard, but he has no time to investigate the cause . . . until at last the weight becomes unendurable, and he is forced to stop and see what is the matter—whereas he should have given heed to the claims of the spirit at the first, and in a brief prayer taken the

"weight" to God, refusing all pressure from the foe.

(2) He should be able to read his spirit, and know at once when it is out of cooperation with the Holy Spirit, quickly refusing all attacks which are drawing his spirit out of the poise of fellowship with God.

(3) He should know when his spirit is touched by the poison of the spirits of evil*—by the injection, for instance, of sadness, soreness, complaint, grumbling, fault-finding, touchiness, bitterness, feeling hurt, jealousy, etc.—all direct from the enemy to the *spirit.* He should resist all sadness, gloom and grumbling injected into his spirit—for the victory life of a freed spirit means joyfulness (Gal. 5:22). Believers ordinarily think that sadness has to do with their disposition, and so yield to it without a thought of resistance or reasoning out the cause. If they were asked if a man with a strong disposition to steal should yield to it, they would at once answer "no"; yet they yield to other "dispositions" less manifestly wrong without a question.

In the stress of conflict, when the believer finds that the enemy succeeds in reaching his spirit with any of these "fiery darts," he should know how to pray immediately against the attack, asking God to destroy the causes of it. It should be noted that this touching of the spirit by the various things just named is not a manifestation of the "works of the flesh"—assuming the believer is one who knows the life after the spirit—but they will quickly reach the sphere of the flesh if not recognized and dealt with in sharp refusal and resistance.

(4) He should know when his spirit is in the right position of dominance over soul and body, and not driven beyond due measure by the exigencies of conflict or environment. There are three conditions of the spirit which the believer should be able to discern and

---

* Their "fiery darts" (Eph. 6:16), to be quenched by the shield of faith.

deal with:

(*a*) The spirit depressed, *i.e.*, crushed or "down."
(*b*) The spirit in its right position, in poise and calm control.
(*c*) The spirit drawn out beyond "poise," when it is in strain, or driven, or in "flight."

When the man walks after the spirit, and discerns it to be in either of the wrong conditions, he knows how to "lift" it when it is depressed; and how to check the overaction by a quiet act of his volition when it is drawn out of poise by over-eagerness, or the drive of spiritual foes.

Some Light on True Guidance After the Spirit

As to "guidance," the believer should understand that when there is no action in his spirit, he should use his mind. If in everything there must be the "Amen" in the spirit, there is no use for the brain at all, but *the spirit does not always speak.* There are times when it should be left in abeyance. In all guidance the mind decides the course of action—not only from the feeling in the spirit but by the light in the mind.

In coming to a decision, the deciding is an act of mind and will, based upon either the mental process of reasoning or the sense of the spirit, or both, *i.e.*:

(1) Decision by mental process, *reasoning*, or
(2) Decision by *sense* of the spirit; *i.e.*, movement, impelling; drawing or restraint; spirit as if "dead"—no response; contraction of spirit; openness of spirit; fullness of spirit; compression of spirit; burden on spirit; wrestling in spirit; resisting in spirit.*

* See Acts 18:5; 19:21; 20:22.

God has three ways of communicating His will to men. By (1) vision to the mind, which is very rare; (2) understanding by the mind; and (3) consciousness to the spirit, that is, by light to the mind and consciousness in spirit. In true guidance, spirit and mind are of one accord, and the intelligence is not in rebellion against the leading in the spirit—as it is so often in counterfeit guidance by evil spirits, when the man is *compelled to act* in obedience to what he thinks is of God, supernaturally given, and fears to disobey.

This all refers to guidance from the subjective standpoint, but it must be emphasized in addition that *all true guidance from God is in harmony with the Scriptures.* The "understanding" of the will of God by the mind depends upon the mind being saturated with the knowledge of the written Word; and true "consciousness in the spirit" depends upon its union with Christ through the indwelling Spirit of God.

The mind should never be dropped into abeyance. The human spirit can be influenced by the mind, therefore the believer should keep his mind in purity, and unbiased, as well as having an unbiased will. Passivity can be produced by seeking for a "leading" in the spirit all day, when there may be no action in the spirit to go by. When there is no movement, or "draw," or "leading" in the spirit, then the mind should be used in reliance upon the promise of God: "The meek will He guide in judgment" (Ps. 25:9). An example of this use of his mind when Paul had no consciousness in his spirit of any special guidance from God is clearly given by him when he wrote to the Corinthians that in one matter he had commandment (1 Cor. 7:10), but in another he said, "I have no commandment of the Lord, but I give my judgment" (1 Cor. 7:25). In the one case he had the guidance through his spirit; in the other he used his mind, and clearly said so—see verse 40: "after my judgment."

Through ignorance a large majority of believers walk "after the soul," *i.e.*, their mind and emotions, and think they are "walking after the spirit." The satanic forces know this right well, and use all their wiles to draw the believer to live in his soul or body, sometimes flashing visions to the mind, or giving exquisite sensations of joy, buoyancy of life, etc., to the body—and the believer "walks after the soul" and "after the body" as he follows these things, believing that he is following the Spirit of God.

Depending upon supernatural things given from outside or on spiritual experiences in the sense realm checks the inward spiritual life through the spirit. By these experiences of the senses, instead of living in the true sphere of the spirit the believer is drawn out to live in the outer man of his body; and ceasing to act from his center, he is caught by the outer workings of the supernatural in his environment and loses the inner cooperation with God. The devil's scheme is therefore to make the believer cease walking after the spirit, and to draw him out into the realm of soul or body. Then the spirit, which is the organ of the Holy Spirit in conflict against a spiritual foe, drops into abeyance and is ignored, because the believer is occupied with the sense-experience. It is then practically out of action, either for guidance, or power in service, or conflict.

The Counterfeit of the Human Spirit

Evil spirits then seek to create a counterfeit of the spirit. If the believer is ignorant of the tactics of the enemy in this way, he lets go the true spirit-action (or allows it to sink into disuse) and follows the counterfeit spiritual feelings, thinking he is walking after the spirit all the time.

When this true spirit-action ceases, the evil spirits suggest that God now guides through the "renewed mind," which is an attempt to hide their workings and the man's disuse of his spirit. Upon the cessation of the spirit's cooperation with the Holy Spirit, with counterfeit "spirit" feelings taking place in the body, what follows is counterfeit light to the mind, reasoning, judging, etc.—the man thus walking after *mind and body*, and not after the spirit, with the true illumination of the mind which comes from the full operation of the Holy Spirit.

To further interfere with the true spirit life, the deceiving spirits seek to counterfeit the action of the spirit in burden and anguish. This they do by first giving a fictitious "divine love" to the person, the faculty receiving it being the affections. When these affections are grasped fully by the deceivers, the *sense* of love passes away, and the man thinks he has lost God and all communion with God. Then follow feelings of constraint and restraint, which will develop into acute suffering—which the believer thinks is in the *spirit*, and of God. Now he *goes by these feelings*, calling them "anguish in the spirit," "groaning in the spirit," etc., while the deceiving spirits, through these sufferings given by them in the affections, compel the man to do their will.

All physical consciousness of supernatural things, and even undue consciousness of natural things, should be refused, as this diverts the mind from walking after the spirit and sets it upon the bodily sensations. Physical consciousness is also an obstacle to the continuous concentration of the mind, and in a spiritual believer an "attack" of physical "consciousness" made use of by the enemy may break concentration of the mind and bring a cloud upon the spirit. The body should be kept calm, and under full control; excessive laughter should be avoided, and all "rushing" which rouses the physical life to the extent of dominating mind and spirit. Believers who desire to be "spiritual" and of "full age" in the life in God should avoid excess, extravagance, and extremes in all things (see 1 Cor. 9:25–27).

Because of the domination of the physical part of the man, and the emphasis placed upon supernatural experiences in the body, the body is made to do the work of the spirit and is forced into a prominence which hides the true spirit life. It *feels* the pressure, feels the conflict, and *thus becomes the locus of the sense instead of it being the spirit.* These believers do not perceive *where* they feel. If they are questioned as to *where* they "feel," they cannot answer. They should learn to discriminate, and know how to discern the feelings of the spirit, which are neither emotional (soulish) nor physical. (See, for example, Mark 8:12; John 13:21; Acts 18:5, KJV.)

The spirit may be likened to an electric light. If the man's spirit is in contact with the Spirit of God, it is full of light; apart from Him it is in darkness. Indwelt by Him, "the spirit of man is the lamp of the Lord" (Prov. 20:27). The possibilities and potentialities of the human spirit are only known when the spirit is joined to Christ and, united to Him, is made strong to stand against the powers of darkness.

The great need of the Church is to know and understand the laws of the spirit, so as to co-work with the Spirit of God in fulfilling the purpose of God through His people. But the lack of knowledge of the spirit life has given the deceiving spirits of Satan the opportunity for the deceptions of which we have spoken in the previous pages of this book.

CHAPTER 8

Victory in Conflict

How may a believer be victorious over the powers of darkness? How may he have authority and victory over wicked spirits rather than be mastered by them? This is the question we shall seek to answer in this chapter—but not simply for the sake of the individual believer. Any Christian who has come to recognize the devices of the enemy in his own life, and has learned the way of deliverance, will be deeply concerned that others also be set free. "Authority . . . over all the power of the enemy" (Luke 10:19)—what a wonderful goal, for oneself and for others!

A believer must learn to walk in personal victory over the devil at every point if he is to have the fullest victory over the powers of darkness. For this, he needs to know the Lord Christ in all the aspects of His name and character, so as to draw upon His power in *living union with Him*. The believer must also learn to know the *Adversary* in *his* various workings, as described in his names and character, so that he may be able to discern the presence of Satan and all his wicked spirits wheresoever they may be—either in attacks upon himself, upon others, or in their working as "world-rulers" of the darkness in the world.

Victory Over Satan as Tempter

Victory over the devil as a tempter, and all his temptations—whether direct or indirect—must be learned by the believer from personal experience. He must remember that not all "temptations" are recognizable as temptations, nor are they always visible—for half their power lies in their being hidden. A believer often thinks that he will be as conscious of the approach of temptation as he is of a person coming into the room. Hence the children of God are only fighting a small proportion of the devil's workings: that is, only what they are *conscious of* as supernatural workings of evil.

Because their knowledge of the devil's character and methods of working is limited and circumscribed, many true children of God only recognize "temptation" when the nature of the thing presented is visibly evil, and accords with their *limited knowledge* of evil. So they do not recognize the tempter and his temptations when they come under the guise of lawful and apparent "good."

When the Prince of Darkness and his emissaries come as angels of light they clothe themselves in *light*, which, in their case, stands for *evil*. It is a "light" which is really darkness. They come in the guise of good—for darkness is opposed to light, ignorance is opposed to knowledge, falsehood is opposed to truth. Darkness is a term we ordinarily apply to evil morality and moral darkness. Hence the believer may need to discern evil spirits in the realm of the supposed good. That which comes to them as "light" actually may be darkness. The apparent "good" may be really evil. And so the apparent "help" which the believer clings to may be really a hindrance.

There needs to be a choice between good and evil made perpetually by every man. The Hebrew priests of old were specially called to discern and teach the people the difference between "the holy and the common," "the unclean and the clean" (Ezek. 44:23). Yet is the Church of Christ today able thus to discern what is good and what is evil? Does she not continually fall into the snare of calling good "evil," and evil "good"? Because the thoughts of God's people are so often governed by ignorance and limited knowledge, they can call the works of God "devilish" and the works of the devil "divine." For they are not taught the necessity of learning to discern the difference between "the unclean and the clean," nor how to decide for themselves what is of God and what is of the devil—although they are unknowingly compelled to make a choice every moment of the day.

Neither do all believers know that they have a choice between good and good, *i.e.*, between the lesser and the greater good—and the devil often entangles them here.

VARIOUS KINDS OF TEMPTATION

There are seen temptations, and temptations in the unseen. Physical temptations, soulish temptations, spiritual temptations; direct and indirect temptations—as with Christ when He was directly tempted in the wilderness, or indirectly through Peter. The believer must not only resist the devil when he tempts openly, or attacks consciously, but *by constant prayer he must bring to light Satan's hidden and covered temptations,* knowing that he is a tempter, and therefore is always planning temptation for the believer. Those who thus, by prayer, bring to light these hidden workings are, by experience, widening their horizon in knowledge of his work as a tempter, and becoming better able to co-work with the Spirit of God in the deliverance of others from the power of the enemy; for in order to be victorious over the powers of darkness, it is essential to be able to recognize what they are doing. Paul, on one occasion, did not say "circumstances" but "Satan hindered me" (1 Thess. 2:18), because he was able to recognize when circumstances, or the Holy Spirit (Acts 16:6), or Satan, hindered or restrained him in his life and service.

There are degrees also in the results of temptation. After the wilderness temptation, which settled vast and eternal issues, the devil left Christ, but he returned to Him again and again with other degrees of temptation (John 12:27; Matt. 22:15), both direct and indirect.

The Difference Between "Temptation" and "Attacks"

There is also a difference between the "temptations" and "attacks" of a tempter, as may again be seen in the life of Christ. "Temptation" is a scheme or a plot, or compulsion on the part of the tempter to cause another to do evil, whether consciously or unconsciously; but an attack is an onslaught on the person, either in life, character or circumstances: for example, the devil made an onslaught on the Lord through the villagers when they sought to hurl Him over the brow of the hill (Luke 4:29); when His family brought a charge of insanity against Him (Mark 3:21); and when He was charged with demon possession by His enemies (John 10:20; Matt. 12:24).

Temptation, moreover, means suffering, as we see again in the life of Christ, for it is written, "He *suffered* being tempted" (Heb. 2:18), and believers must not think they will reach a period when they will not feel the suffering of temptation; this is a wrong conception, which gives ground to the enemy for tormenting and attacking them without cause.

Prayer Brings Hidden Temptations to Light

For perpetual victory, therefore, the believer must unceasingly be on guard against the Tempter and his agents, praying that all hidden temptations will be revealed as such. The degree to which one understands Satan's workings will be determined by the degree of victory experienced, for "in vain is the net spread in the sight of any bird." We have given in preceding chapters much knowledge needed by the believer if he is to gain victory over every aspect of a tempter's workings, but especially does he require the power of discrimination between what is temptation from a seducer working upon the uncrucified "old man," temptation through the things of the world (1 John 2:15–16; 5:4–5), and temptation direct from the spirits of evil.

In temptation the crucial point is for the tempted one to know whether the tempting is the work of an evil spirit or from the evil nature. This can be discerned only by the experiential knowledge of Romans 6 as the basis of one's life. Temptation from the fallen nature should be dealt with on the foundation of "Reckon ye also yourselves to be dead unto sin, but alive unto God in Christ Jesus" (Rom. 6:11), and practical obedience to the resulting command, "*Let not sin reign* in your mortal body." In the hour of temptation to sin—to visible, known sin—the believer should take his stand on Romans 6:6 as his deliberate position of faith, and in obedience to Romans 6:11 declare his undeviating choice and attitude as "death to sin, in death-union with Christ." If this choice is the expression of his real will, and the temptation to sin does not cease, he should then deal with the spirits of evil who may be seeking to awaken sinful desires (Jas. 1:14) or to *counterfeit them.* For they can counterfeit the old nature in evil desire, evil thoughts, evil words, evil presentations—and many honest believers think they are battling with the workings of the old nature when these things are given by evil spirits. But if the believer is not standing actively on Romans 6, the "counterfeits" are not necessary, for the old fallen creation is always open to be wrought upon by the powers of darkness.

Victory Over Satan as Accuser

The difference between the accusations of the enemy

and his temptations is that the latter is an effort on his part to compel or draw the man into sin, and the former is a charge of transgression. Temptation is an effort to cause the man to transgress the law; accusation is an effort to place the believer in the guilty position of having transgressed the law. Evil spirits want the man to be wrong so that they may accuse and punish him for being wrong. "Accusation" can be a counterfeit of conviction—the true conviction of the Spirit of God. It is important that the believer should know, when the charge of transgression is made, whether it is a divine conviction or a satanic accusation.

Yes, the devil may accuse a person when he is truly guilty. But he may also accuse a person when he is not guilty—endeavoring to make his accusations seem like a conviction from the man's own conscience. Evil spirits are thus able to infuse a sense of guilt.

A genuine sin originates from the evil nature within—a result of the Fall. It is not a transgression forced into the personality from without—something involuntary. How can the believer tell if evil spirits are at the back of an involuntary sin? If the man is right with God, standing on Romans 6 with no deliberate yielding to known sin, then any accusation of sin coming back again unaccountably may be dealt with as from evil spirits.

The believer must therefore never accept an accusation—or a charge, *supernaturally made*—of having transgressed unless he is fully convinced, by his own knowledge and clear decision, that he has sinned; for if he accepts the charge when innocent, he will suffer as much as if he had really transgressed. He must also be on guard to refuse any *compulsory* drive to "confession" of sin to others, which may be the forcing of the enemy to pass on his lying accusations.

THE BELIEVER SHOULD MAINTAIN NEUTRALITY TO ACCUSATIONS UNTIL THEIR SOURCE IS PROVED

The believer should maintain neutrality to accusations until he is sure of their real source, and if the man knows he is guilty he should at once go to God on the ground of 1 John 1:9 and refuse to be lashed by the devil—as he is not the judge of God's children, nor is he deputized as God's messenger to make the charge of wrong. The Holy Spirit alone is commissioned by God to convict of sin.

The steps in the working of evil spirits in their accusations and false charges are these, *when the believer accepts their accusations:*

(1) The believer thinks and believes he is guilty.
(2) Evil spirits cause him to feel guilty.
(3) They cause him, then, to appear guilty.
(4) They cause him then to be actually guilty *through believing their lies.* It matters not whether he is guilty or not in the first instance.

Malicious spirits try to make a person feel guilty by their nagging accusations, so as to make him act or appear guilty before others—at the same moment flashing or suggesting to others the very things about which they are accusing him without cause. All such "feelings" should be investigated by the believer. Feeling wrong is not sufficient ground for one to say he is wrong. He should ask, "Is the feeling right?" He may feel wrong and be right, or feel right and be wrong. Therefore he should investigate and examine the question honestly, "Am I wrong?"

"FEELINGS" INJECTED BY EVIL SPIRITS

There are physical, soulish and spiritual "feelings." Evil spirits can inject feelings into any of these departments. Their aim is to move the man by "feelings"—to substitute these for the action of his mind, so that the believer is governed by the deceiving spirits through his feelings. Also to substitute feelings for the conscience in its recognition of right and wrong. Then if believers "feel" they can do a thing, they will do it without asking whether it be right or wrong—if it is not visibly sinful. So for victory over the deceitful enemy it is essential that the children of God cease to be guided by "feelings" in their actions.

Likewise, if believers in any course of action "feel relief," they may conclude the sense of relief is a sign that they have been doing God's will. But it is natural for a man to get rest when his work is done, not only in the spiritual but in ordinary life. A sense of relief in any line of action is no criterion that it is in the will of God. The action must be judged by itself, and not merely by its effects upon the doer. Peace and rest and relief are no proof at all of being in God's will. Some believers also think that if they do some action that the devil wants them to do they will "feel condemned" at once, but they overlook the fact that Satan can give pleasant feelings.

There are innumerable varieties of feelings caused by evil spirits; also countless sorts of attacks and false suggestions. These call forth all the spiritual discernment of the believer, and his understanding of spiritual things, in order to recognize them.

The Need of Differentiating Accusation From True Conviction

The devil very quickly becomes an accuser even if he does not succeed in getting a person to yield to his temptations. As we have seen, deceiving spirits can cause apparent "sin" to be manifested to the consciousness of a believer, and then will lash and accuse the man for their own workings. They counterfeit some sin, which may be called with sadness "my besetting sin," in the believer's life; and as long as it is believed to be sin *from the evil nature*, no "confessing" or seeking victory over it will cause it to pass away. They can also hide behind real sin.

A sense of guiltlessness does not necessarily lead to absolute happiness, for even with the peace of conscious innocence there may be suffering, and the suffering may have its source in some sin which is not known. Walking by known light, and measuring guiltlessness by one's cognizance of sin, is very dangerous for anyone who desires a fathomless peace, for it leads only to superficial rest—which may be disturbed at any moment by the attacks of the Accuser, who will direct his darts at a joint in the armor of peace which is hidden from the believer's view.

For obtaining victory over the Deceiver's accusing spirits, spiritual believers should, therefore, understand clearly whether any consciousness of sin is the result of real transgression or is caused by evil spirits. If the believer accepts the consciousness of sin as from himself when it is not, he at once leaves his position of being "dead to sin" and reckons himself alive to it. This explains why many who have truly known victory over sin by the "reckon" of Romans 6:11 later surrender their basis and lose the position of victory—because the Accuser has counterfeited some manifestation of "self" or "sin" and then accused the man of it, with the taunt that "Romans 6 does not work." This can cause one to fall into confusion and condemnation, as into a pit of miry clay and darkness.

The Need for Unflinching Warfare Against Sin

On the other hand, if the believer in the slightest degree is tempted to treat sin lightly, or attribute it to evil spirits when it is from himself, he is equally on false ground, and lays himself open to the old fallen nature regaining mastery over him with redoubled force. The warfare against Satan must be accompanied with a vigorous, unflinching warfare against sin. Any known sin must not be tolerated for a moment. Whether it be from the fallen nature or from evil spirits forcing it into the man, *it must be cast off and put away*, on the basis of Romans 6:6 and 12.

Two misconceptions which give great advantage to the watching enemy are the thoughts in many believers' minds that if a Christian commits sin (1) he will at once know it himself, or (2) that God will tell him. They therefore expect God to tell them when they are right or wrong, instead of seeking light and knowledge according to John 3:21.

Believers seeking victory over all the deceptions of the enemy must take an active part in dealing with sin. Based upon a wrong conception of "death," they may have thought that God would remove sin out of their lives for them—with the result that they have failed actively to co-work with Him in dealing with evil within and in their environment: in others and in the world.

For a life of perpetual victory over Satan as Accuser, it is very important that the believer should understand and detect any inconsistency between the attitude of the *will* and the actions in his life. He should judge himself from his *actions* as well as from his will and motives. For instance, a person is charged with doing a certain thing, which he at once denies, because the action does not agree with his *will-attitude;* and therefore, he says, it is impossible that he should have acted or spoken in the way stated. The believer is judging himself by his own inner standpoint of will and motives, and not by actions as well as by his will (1 Cor. 11:31).

On the Godward side, the cleansing power of the blood of Christ (1 John 1:7) is needed continuously for those who seek to walk in the light, cleansing themselves from all defilement of flesh and spirit, perfecting holiness in the fear of God (2 Cor. 7:1).

The devil as an accuser also works indirectly through others, inciting them to make accusations which he wants the man to accept as true, and thus open the door to him to *make* them true. Or he accuses the believer to others by "visions" or "revelations" about him, which causes them to misjudge him. In any case, whatever may come to the believer from man or devil, LET HIM MAKE USE OF IT FOR PRAYER, and by prayer turn all accusations into steps to victory.

VICTORY OVER SATAN AS A LIAR

The devil is a liar: "He was a murderer from the beginning, and stood not in the truth, because there is no truth in him. When he speaketh a lie, he speaketh of his own; for he is a liar, and the father thereof" (John 8:44). This does not mean that the enemy never tells the truth, but his truth has the objective of getting the believer involved in evil; *e.g.*, when the spirit of divination spoke the truth that Paul and Silas were the servants of God, it was to suggest the lie that Paul and Silas derived their power from the same source as the girl under the evil spirit's power. The devil and his wicked spirits will speak, or use, ninety-nine parts of truth to float one lie, but Paul was not deceived by the witness of a soothsaying prophetess acknowledging their divine authority. He discerned the wicked spirit and its purpose, exposed it, and cast it out.

Even so must the believer be able to triumph over Satan as a liar, and be able to recognize his lies, and those of lying spirits, in whatever form they are presented to him. This he does by knowing the truth, and using the weapon of truth.

VICTORY OVER FALSEHOOD BY TRUTH

There is no way of victory over falsehood but by truth. To have victory over the devil as a liar, and over his lies, the believer must be determined always to know the truth and speak the truth about everything—in himself, in others, and all around him.

Satan the liar, through his lying spirits, persistently pours lies on the believer all day long: lies into his thoughts about himself, his feelings, his condition, his environment; lies misinterpreting everything in himself, and around him—about others with whom he is in contact; lies about the past and the future; lies about God; and lies about the devil himself, magnifying his power and his authority. To have victory over this persistent stream of lies from the father of lies, the believer must fight (1) with the weapon of God's truth in the written Word, and (2) with truth about facts in himself, others, and circumstances. As the believer increasingly triumphs over the devil as a liar, he grows better able to discern his lies, and is equipped to strip away the covering for others.

Victory Over Satan as a Counterfeiter

The devil is a counterfeiter, a false "angel of light": "Even Satan himself fashioneth himself into an angel of light," and his "ministers" ("false apostles, deceitful workers," 2 Cor. 11:13) also fashion themselves as "ministers of righteousness" (2 Cor. 11:14–15). This aspect of victory over Satan runs on the same lines as the preceding ones; *i.e.*, by the knowledge of truth, enabling the believer to recognize the lies of Satan when he presents himself under the guise of light.

Light is the very nature of God Himself. To recognize darkness when clothed in light—supernatural light—requires deep knowledge of the true light, and a power to discern the innermost sources of things that in appearance look Godlike and beautiful. The main attitude for this aspect of victory over the Adversary is a settled position of neutrality to all supernatural workings, until the believer knows what is of God. If any experience is accepted without question, how can its divine origin be guaranteed? The basis of acceptance or rejection must be *knowledge*. The believer must *know*, and he cannot know without examination; nor will he "examine" unless he maintains the attitude of "Believe not every spirit" until he has "tested" and proved what is of God.

VICTORY OVER SATAN AS A HINDERER

The devil is a hinderer: "We would fain have come unto you . . . but Satan hindered us" (1 Thess. 2:18), wrote Paul, who was able to discern between the hindering of Satan and the restraining of the Holy Spirit of God (Acts 16:6). This again means knowledge, and power to discern Satan's workings and schemings and the obstacles he places in the paths of the children of God—obstacles which look so "natural" and so like "providence" that numbers meekly bow their heads and allow the Hinderer to prevail.

Power to discern comes (1) by knowledge that Satan can hinder; (2) by observing the objective of the hindrances, and (3) by close observations of his methods along this line. For example, is it God or Satan withholding money from missionaries preaching the gospel of Calvary, and giving abundance to those who preach error and teachings which are the outcome of the spirit of antichrist? Is it God or Satan hindering a believer by circumstances or sickness from vital service important to the Church of God? Is it God or Satan urging a family to move their residence, without reasonable grounds, to another neighborhood, when it involves the removal of another member from a strategic vantage-ground of service to God, with no other worker to take his place? Is it God or Satan leading Christians to put first their (1) health, (2) comfort, (3) social position in their decisions, rather than the needs and the exigencies of the kingdom of God? Is it God or Satan who hinders service for God through members of a family making objections, or through troubles in business which give no time for such service, or through property losses, etc.? Knowledge of the Hinderer means victory by prayer over his schemes and workings. The believer should therefore know his wiles.

Victory Over Satan as a Murderer

The devil is a murderer (John 15:44). Satan as the Prince of Death watches every occasion to take the life of servants of God—if in any wise he can get them to fulfill conditions which enable him to do so: (1) by their willful insistence on going into danger without being sent of God; (2) by trapping them into danger through visions or supernatural guidance, drawing them into actions which enable him to work behind the laws of nature for destroying their lives. That is what Satan tried to do with Christ in the wilderness temptation: "Throw Thyself down," he said, and then quoted Scripture to show that the Lord had scriptural warrant for believing that angel hands would bear Him up and not allow Him to fall (Luke 4:11). But the Son of God recognized the Tempter and the Murderer. He knew that His life would end as a man were He to give occasion to the malignant hate of Satan by one step out of God's will, and that the Deceiver would not propose anything, however apparently innocent or seemingly for God's glory, unless some great scheme for his own ends was deeply hidden in his proposition.

Christ now holds "the keys of death and of Hades" (Rev. 1:18), and "him that hath the power of death, that is, the devil" (Heb. 2:14, mg.) cannot exercise his power *without permission*. But when the children of God, knowingly or unknowingly, fulfill the conditions which give Satan ground to attack their physical lives, the Lord with "the keys of death" works according to law, and does not save them—*unless by the weapon of prayer* they enable God to interpose and give them victory over the law of death, as well as the law of sin, through "the law of the Spirit of life in Christ Jesus" (Rom. 8:2).

"The last enemy that shall be destroyed is death." Death is therefore an enemy—to be recognized as an enemy and to be resisted as an enemy. The believer may lawfully "desire to depart and be with Christ" (Phil. 1:23), but ought never to desire death merely as an end of "trouble." He should not let the lawful desire to be with Christ make him *yield to death when he is needed for the service of the Church of God.* "To abide in the flesh is needful for you," wrote the Apostle Paul to the Philippians, therefore "I *know* that I shall abide" (Phil. 1:24–25).

Believers Should Resist Death as an Enemy

The will of the believer "willing" physical death gives the Adversary power of death over that one, and no believer should yield to a "desire to die" until he knows beyond question that God has released him from further service to His people. That a believer is "ready to die" is a very small matter; he must be also ready to live, until he is sure that his lifework is finished. God does not harvest His corn until it is ripe, and His redeemed children should be "garnered as a shock of corn in its season."

It is ofttimes the Prince of Death as a murderer—working through the ignorance of God's children as to (1) his power, (2) the conditions by which they give him power, and (3) the victory of prayer by which they can resist his power—who cuts off God's soldiers from the battlefield. It is Satan as a murderer who gives "visions of glory" and "longings to die" to workers of value to the Church of God, so that they yield to death even in days of active service, and slowly fade away.

Believers who would have victory over Satan at every

point must resist his attack on the body, as well as on the spirit and mind. They must seek knowledge of God's laws for the body, so as to obey those laws and give no occasion to Satan to slay them. They should know the place of the body in the spiritual life: (1) its prominence, and yet (2) its obscurity. Paul said, "I keep under my body"—I discipline it. They must understand that the more knowledge they have of the devices and power of the Adversary, and of the fullness of the Calvary victory within their reach for complete victory over him, the more he will plan to injure them. The whole of his schemes against God's children may be summed up under three heads: (1) To *cause them to sin*, as he tempted Christ in the wilderness; (2) To *slander them*, as Christ was slandered by family and foes; (3) To *slay them*, as Christ was slain at Calvary, when, by the direct permission of God, the hour and power of darkness gathered around Him, and He by the hands of wicked men was crucified and slain (Acts 2:23).

As the believer gains victories over Satan and his deceiving and lying spirits by thus recognizing, resisting and triumphing over them in their varied workings, his strength of spirit to conquer them grows stronger, and he will become more and more equipped to set forth the truth of the finished work of Calvary as sufficient for victory over sin and Satan. Done in the power and authority of Christ by the Holy Spirit, this will set others free from their power.

It must, of course, be clearly recognized that victory over Satan in these aspects will not be without great onslaughts from him and sharp conflict, which may well be called "the evil day" (Eph. 6:13).

THE VALUE AND PURPOSE OF "REFUSING"

It is essential that believers should understand the value of the act of refusal, and the expression of it. Briefly: REFUSAL IS THE OPPOSITE OF ACCEPTANCE. Evil spirits have gained by the believer giving them (1) ground, (2) right of way, (3) use of one's faculties, etc., and they lose when this is all withdrawn from them. What was given to the enemy by misconception and ignorance, and given with the consent of the will, stands as ground for them to work on and through—until, by the same action of the will, the "giving" is revoked, specifically and generally. The will in the past was unknowingly put for evil, and it must now be put unceasingly against it.

Once understood, the principle is very simple. The choice of the will gives; the choice of the will withdraws or nullifies the previous giving. The value and purpose of refusing stands the same toward God and toward Satan. The man gives to God, or refuses to give. He takes from God, or refuses to take. He gives to evil spirits—unknowingly or not—and he refuses to give. He finds he has given to them unwittingly, and he nullifies it by an act of withdrawal and refusal.

The Relation of Fresh Ground Given to the Victory in Conflict

The relationship between aggressive warfare and freshly discovered "ground" given to deceiving spirits is important. Every new ground discovered as given to them means, when refused, a renewed liberation of the spirit. This produces deepened enmity to the foe as his subtle deceptions are increasingly exposed, and consequently more war upon Satan and his minions. It means more deliverance from their power, and less ground in the believer as he realizes that "symptoms," "effects" and "manifestations" are not abstract things but revelations of active, personal agencies, against whom he must war persistently.

Moreover, all growth in this practical knowledge means increased protection against the deceiving enemy. As new ground is revealed, and fresh truth about the powers of darkness and the way of victory over them is understood, the truth delivers from their deceptions, and hence protects the believer—up to the extent of his knowledge—from further deception. He finds in experience that as soon as the truth ceases to operate by his active use of it, he is open to attack from the watching foe, who ceaselessly plans against him. For example, should the believer who has been undeceived cease to use the truth of (1) the existence of evil spirits, (2) their persistent watching to deceive him again, (3) the need for perpetual resistance and fight against them, (4) the keeping of his spirit in purity and strength in cooperation with the Spirit of God, and other truths parallel with these—the knowledge of which he has gained through so much suffering—he will sink down again into passivity, and possibly deeper depths of deception. For the Holy Spirit *needs the believer's use of truth* to work with in energizing and strengthening him for conflict and victory, and does not guard him from the enemy apart from his cooperation in watching and prayer.

PERSISTENT REFUSAL OF GROUND TO EVIL SPIRITS

The way to refuse, and what to refuse, is of primary importance in the hour of conflict. As we have seen, the believer needs to maintain an active attitude, and, when necessary, the expression of refusal continually and persistently. This presupposes, of course, his standing in faith upon the foundation of his identification in death with Christ at Calvary.

In the hour of conflict, lest there might have been new ground given to evil spirits unknowingly—by accepting something from them, or believing some lie they have suggested to the mind—the believer should refuse all the possible things whereby they may have gained a new footing. The believer himself will know, from his past experience, most of the ways by which the deceiving spirits have hitherto gained advantage over him; and he will instinctively turn to the points of refusal which have been of the most service to him in his fight to freedom. The refusing in this way takes ground from them in many directions. The wider the scope covered by the act and attitude of refusal, the more thoroughly is the believer separating himself from the deceiving spirits—who can only hold their ground by the consent of his will. By refusing all he once accepted from them he can become comparatively clear of ground given to them, so far as his choice and attitude is concerned.

Refusal an Aggressive Weapon in Conflict

In the hour of conflict, when the forces of darkness are pressing upon the believer, the expression of his active refusal becomes an aggressive act of warfare against them, as well as a defensive weapon. It is then that, instead of sinking down in fear and despair when the enemy assaults the city, the will at the center of "Mansoul"* issues forth in aggressive resistance against the foe, by declaring its attitude against him. The battle turns upon the choice of the will in the citadel being maintained, in unshaken refusal to yield to or admit any one of the attacking spirits of evil. The whole power of God, by the Holy Spirit, will be at the back of the active resistance of the man in his attitude of refusal toward the enemy.

It is important to understand the effectiveness of this refusal of the will on the part of the undeceived believer. It is a barrier against the foe. We must recognize that our outer man, in both its "feelings" and nervous system, still bears scars long after its deliverance from the pit of deception into which it had been

* As in Bunyan's *The Holy War.*

beguiled. When once the wall of the outer man has been broken into by supernatural forces of evil, it is not quickly rebuilt. Believers who are emerging from deception should therefore know that there is power in aggressively turning upon the enemy at the moment of his attacking them—actively expressing their choice and will in regard to him. This aggressive action also becomes a defensive one.

The same weapon of *refusing* works in many phases of the conflict. For example, in speaking or writing, if the believer is conscious of difficulties, obstacles, or interference in what he is doing, he should at once refuse all ideas, thoughts, suggestions, visions (*i.e.*, pictures to the mind), words, impressions, that the spirits of evil may be seeking to insert or press upon him, so that he may be able to cooperate with the Holy Spirit and have a clarified mind for the carrying out of God's will.

I say it again: The believer, by his refusal and resistance against supernatural attempts to interfere with his outer man, will be actively resisting the powers of darkness, while he seeks to co-work with the Holy Spirit within his spirit. At first this means much conflict, but as he maintains active resistance and increasingly closes his whole being to the spirits of evil, and is on the alert to recognize and refuse their workings, his union with the Risen Lord deepens, his spirit grows strong, his vision becomes pure, his mental faculties are clear enough to realize a perpetual victory over the foes who once had him in their oppressive power.

He must then be especially on guard against what may be described as the "double counterfeits" of the deceiving spirits. That is, the counterfeits offered by the enemy in connection with attacks upon himself. For example, the devil attacks him manifestly and openly, so that he clearly knows it to be an onslaught of the spirit-beings of evil. He prays, resists, gets through to victory in his will and spirit. Then comes a "great feeling" of peace and rest, which may be as much an attack as the original onslaught, but more subtle and liable to mislead the believer if he is not on guard. The enemy, by suddenly retreating and ceasing the furious attack, hopes by this stratagem to gain the advantage which he failed to obtain at the first.

Fighting from Principle

It is essential to understand how to fight "in cold blood," so to speak: *i.e.*, wholly apart from feelings of any kind; for the believer may *feel* it is victory when it is defeat, and vice versa. All dependence upon feeling and acting from impulse must be put aside in this warfare. Some can only recognize "conflict" when they are emotionally conscious of it; they fight spasmodically, or by accident—when forced to it by necessity. But now the "fight" must be permanent and part of the very life. There needs to be a ceaseless recognition of the forces of darkness "in cold blood"—simply because of knowing what they are—and consequently a "fight from principle." There must be a fight against these unseen foes even when there is nothing to be seen of their presence or workings, remembering that they do not always attack when they can. If they were to attack on some occasions they would lose by it, because that would reveal the character of the thing and its source.

The believer knows that the devil, being by nature a tempter, is always tempting—and therefore he resists from principle. In brief, anyone who desires perpetual victory must understand that it is a question of principle versus feeling and consciousness. There can only be intermittent victory if the warfare is governed by the latter rather than the former. So when the enemy attacks him, the believer will find a strong, primary weapon of victory in declaring deliberately his basic position toward sin and Satan: that he is standing on the Calvary ground of Romans 6:6–11. The person reckoning himself in the present moment to be "dead indeed unto sin, and alive unto God" thereby refuses to yield to sin and Satan in any of the points of attack or causes of the conflict.

As the believer thus declares his position in the hour of conflict and onslaught from the foe, he will often find himself obliged to wrestle in real combat with the invisible enemy. Standing on the finished work of Christ, in death to sin, the spirit of the man becomes liberated for action, and energized to stand against the hierarchic hosts of Satan—the principalities and powers, the world-rulers of the darkness, and the hosts of wicked spirits in the heavenly (or spiritual) sphere.

Wrestling and What It Means

It is possible to wrestle against the powers of darkness only by the spirit. This is a *spiritual* warfare, and can only be understood by the spiritual man—that is, a man who lives by and is governed by his spirit. Evil spirits attack, wrestle with, and resist the believer. Therefore he must fight them, wrestle with them, and resist them. This wrestling is not by means of soul or body, but by means of the spirit; for the lesser cannot wrestle with the higher. Body wrestles with body in the physical realm; in the intellectual realm, soul with soul; and in the spiritual, spirit with spirit. But the powers of darkness attack the three-fold nature of man, and through body or soul seek to reach the spirit of man. If the fight is a mental one, the will should be used in decisive action, quietly and steadily. If it is a spirit fight, all the forces of the spirit should be brought to join the mind. If the spirit is pressed down and unable to resist, however, then there should be a steady mental fight—when the mind, as it were, stretches out its hand to lift up the spirit.

The objective of evil spirits is to get the spirit down, and thus render the believer powerless to take aggressive action against them. Or they may seek to push the spirit beyond its due poise and measure, into an effervescence which carries the believer beyond the control of his volition and mind, and hence off guard against the subtle foe—incapable of exercising proper balance of speech, action, thought, and discrimination—so that under cover they may gain some advantage for themselves. And remember, *a great victory means a great danger*, because when the believer is occupied with it, the devil is scheming how to rob him of it. The hour of victory therefore calls for soberness of mind, and watching unto prayer—for a little over-elation may mean its loss and a long, sore fight back to full victory.

When the spirit triumphs in the wrestling and gains the victory, there breaks out, as it were, a stream from the spirit—an overflow of triumph and resistance against the invisible, but very real, foe. But sometimes in the conflict the enemy succeeds in blocking the spirit through their attack on body or soul.

The spirit needs soul and body for expression; hence the enemy's attacks to close the spirit up, so as to render the man unable actively to resist. When this takes place, the believer thinks that he is "reserved," because he feels "shut up." He has "no voice to refuse." In audible prayer "the words seem empty"; he "feels no effect," and they seem mere "mockery." But the fact is that the spirit is closing up as a result of the wrestling enemy gripping, holding and binding it. The believer must now insist on *expressing himself vocally*, until the spirit breaks through into liberty. This is "the word of testimony" which Revelation 12:11 mentions as part of the tactic for overcoming the dragon. The wrestling believer (1) stands on the ground of the blood of the Lamb, which includes all that the finished work of Calvary means in victory over sin and Satan; (2) he gives the word of his testimony in affirming his attitude to sin and Satan, and the sure, certain victory through Christ; and (3) he lives in the Calvary spirit, with his life surrendered to do the will of God, even unto death.

PRAYER AND PERSONAL CONFLICT

Closely bound up with the wrestling of the spirit is the necessity of prayer—not so much the prayer of petition to a Father as the prayer of one joined in spirit with the Son of God, his will fused with His (John 15:7)—declaring to the enemy the authority of Christ over all their power (Eph. 1:20–23).

Sometimes the believer has to "wrestle" in order to pray; at other times, to pray in order to wrestle. If he cannot "fight" he must pray, and if he cannot pray he must fight. For example, if the believer is conscious of a weight on his spirit, he must get rid of the weight by refusing all the "causes" of the weight—for it is necessary to keep the spirit unburdened to fight, and to retain the power of detection. The delicate spirit-sense becomes dull under "weights" or pressure upon it; hence the enemy's ceaseless tactics to get "burdens" or pressure on the spirit, unrecognized as from the foe, or else recognized and allowed to remain.

The man may feel "bound up" and the cause be in others, for (1) there may be no open spirit or open mind in another disciple to receive from the spirit and mind of the one who feels bound up; (2) there may be no capacity in the other to receive any message of truth; (3) there may be some thought in the mind of the other which is checking the flow of the spirit.

If in the morning the believer finds a "weight" or heaviness on his spirit, and it is not dealt with, he is sure to lose his position of victory through the day. In dealing with weight on the spirit, the moment it is recognized the believer must at once act in spirit, and (1) stand (Eph. 6:14), (2) withstand (Eph. 6:13) and (3) resist (Jas. 4:7) the powers of darkness. Each of these positions requires *spirit-action*, for these words do not describe a "state" or an "attitude," nor an act by soul or body.

To "stand" is a spirit-action repelling an aggressive move of the enemy; to "withstand" is to make an aggressive move against them; and to "resist" is actively to fight with his spirit, even as a man "resists" with his body another who is physically attacking him.

The Wiles of the Devil

The word "wiles" in the original means "methods," and bears in its varied forms the thought of craft, artifice or trickery. To "work wiles" is to outwit, or to methodically go in pursuit.

Satan's war on the saints can be summed up in the phrase "the wiles of the devil." He does not work in the open but always behind cover. The methods of his deceiving spirits are adapted to each one, and they have a skill and cunning gained by years of experience. Generally, the wiles are primarily directed against a person's mind or thoughts, so, unless the believer has yielded to known sin, most of the workings of Satan in his life may be traced back to a wrong thought or belief admitted into his mind and not recognized to be from deceiving spirits. For if a believer thinks that all that Satan does is manifestly bad, Satan has only to clothe himself with "good" to gain full credence with that man. The war, therefore, is a war of deceit and counterfeit, and only those who seek the fullest truth from God about God, Satan, and themselves can stand against the Deceiver's wiles.

Knowing the Wiles of the Devil

The Apostle Paul said that the believer was to be able to stand against the wiles of the devil, and that he was to put on the whole armor for doing this. How can a man stand against a wile if he does not know what the wile is? There is a difference between temptation and wiles—between the principles and working of Satan (and his emissaries) and their wiles; *i.e.*, they themselves are *tempters.* Temptation is not a wile. A wile is the way they scheme to tempt. Paul did not say that the believer must stand against "temptations" or lies, or mention any other specific characteristic of evil spirits; but he must be "able to stand" against their wiles. The spiritual man is to be on guard lest he is caught by their wiles. If these can be detected, then Satan's objective can be frustrated and destroyed. The spiritual man needs the fullest concentration and sagacity of mind for reading quickly his spirit-sense, and detecting the active operations of the foe; he also requires alertness in using the message his spirit conveys to him. A spiritual believer ought to be able to read the sense of his spirit with the same instinctive adroitness as a person recognizes cold by his physical sense when he feels a draft, and then immediately uses his mental faculties for actively protecting himself from it.* So the spiritual man needs to use his spirit-sense in locating and dislodging the foe by prayer.

Again, an "objective" and a "wile" are quite distinct. The wile is a means used by the foe to gain an objective. The evil spirits must use "wiles" to carry out their objective. Their objective is deception, but their "wiles" will be counterfeits. They are liars, but how can they succeed in getting their lies into the mind of a man? They do not need wiles to make themselves liars, but they need the wile to get the lie accepted by the believer.

The wiles of the devil and his emissaries are countless and fitted to the individual believer. If he is to be moved by *suffering* from any course of action detrimental to their interests, they will play upon his sympathies by the suffering they cause to someone near and

* See 1 John 5:18, KJV.

dear to him. Or if he shrinks from personal suffering, they will work upon this to make him change his course. To those who are naturally sympathetic, they will use a counterfeit of love. Those who can be attracted by intellectual things will be drawn from the spiritual sphere by being driven to excessive study, or be given mental attractions of many kinds. While others—those who are oversensitive and conscientious—may be constantly charged with blame for apparently continuous failure. The lying spirits lash the person for what they themselves do, but if the believer understands how to refuse all blame from them he can use their very doings as a weapon against them.

THE ARMOR FOR THE CONFLICT

For this conflict with the powers of darkness the believer must learn by experience how to take and use the armor for the battle, described by the apostle in Ephesians 6. The objective in Ephesians 6 is clearly not victory over sin—this is assumed—but VICTORY OVER SATAN. The call is not to the world, but to the Church. It is a call to stand in armor; to stand in the evil day; to stand against the powers of darkness; to stand after accomplishing the work of overthrowing them—"having overcome all," verse 13, KJV mg.—by the strength given of God.

The armor in detail, as set forth in Ephesians 6, is provided that the child of God should be "*able* to stand" against the wiles of the devil—clearly showing that a believer can be made able to conquer all the principalities and powers of hell if he fulfills the necessary conditions, and uses the armor provided for him.

It must be a *real armor* if it is provided for meeting a *real foe*, and God evidently demands a *real knowledge* of it on the part of the believer—to whom the fact of the provision, the fact of the foe, and the fact of the fight must be as *real facts* as any other facts declared in the

Scriptures. The armored and non-armored believer may be briefly contrasted as follows:

The Armored Christian	*The Non-armored Christian*
Armored with truth.	Open to lies, through ignorance.
Righteousness of life.	Unrighteousness through ignorance.
Making and keeping peace.	Divisions and quarrels.
Self-preservation* and control.	Reckless unwatchfulness.
Faith as a shield.	Doubt and unbelief.
Scriptures in the hand and often memorized.	Relying on reason instead of God's Word.
Prayer without ceasing.	Relying on work without prayer.

The believer who takes up the whole armor of God as a covering and protection against the foe should himself then start walking in victory over the enemy. To do this he must (1) have his spirit indwelt by the Holy Spirit, so that he is strengthened with the might of God to stand unshaken—and be given continuously a "supply of the Spirit of Jesus" to keep his spirit sweet and pure; (2) have his mind renewed (Rom. 12: 2) so that he has his understanding filled with the light of truth (Eph. 1:18), displacing Satan's lies, and destroying the veil with which Satan once held it—the mind being clarified so that he intelligently understands what the will of the Lord is; (3) have his body subservient to the Spirit (1 Cor. 9:25–27), and obedient to the will of God in life and service.

Believer, advance!

---

* Root meaning of the word "salvation" in Ephesians 6:17.
Note. For further light on "temptation" and "accusation," it is suggested that John Bunyan's *Grace Abounding to the Chief of Sinners* should be studied.

APPENDIX

THE ATTITUDE OF THE EARLY FATHERS TO EVIL SPIRITS

TERTULLIAN says, in his *Apology* addressed to the rulers of the Roman Empire:

". . . Let a person be brought before your tribunals who is plainly under demoniacal possession. The wicked spirit, bidden to speak by a follower of Christ, will as readily make the truthful confession that he is a demon as elsewhere he has falsely asserted that he is a god. Or, if you will, let there be produced one of the 'god-possessed,' as they are supposed. If they do not confess, IN THEIR FEAR OF LYING TO A CHRISTIAN, that they are demons, then and there shed the blood of that most impudent follower of Christ.

"ALL THE AUTHORITY AND POWER WE HAVE OVER THEM IS FROM OUR NAMING THE NAME OF CHRIST, AND RECALLING TO THEIR MEMORY THE WOES WITH WHICH GOD THREATENS THEM AT THE HAND OF CHRIST THEIR JUDGE, AND WHICH THEY EXPECT ONE DAY TO OVERTAKE THEM. FEARING CHRIST IN GOD AND GOD IN CHRIST, THEY BECOME SUBJECT TO THE SERVANTS OF GOD AND CHRIST. SO AT ONE TOUCH AND BREATHING, OVERWHELMED BY THE THOUGHT AND REALIZATION OF THOSE JUDGMENT FIRES, THEY LEAVE AT OUR COMMAND THE BODIES THEY HAVE ENTERED, UNWILLING AND DISTRESSED, AND BEFORE YOUR VERY EYES, PUT TO AN OPEN SHAME. . . ."

JUSTIN MARTYR, in his second *Apology* addressed to the Roman Senate, says: "Numberless demoniacs throughout the whole world and in your city, many of our Christian men—exorcising them in the name of

Jesus Christ who was crucified under Pontius Pilate—have healed and do heal, rendering helpless, and driving the possessing demon out of the men, though they could not be cured by all other exorcists, and those who use incantations and drugs."

CYPRIAN expressed himself with equal confidence. After having said that they are evil spirits that inspire the false prophets of the Gentiles, and deliver oracles by always mixing truth with falsehood to prove what they say, he adds: "Nevertheless these evil spirits adjured by the living God IMMEDIATELY OBEY US, SUBMIT TO US, OWN OUR POWER, and are forced to come out of the bodies they possess. . . ."

▼▼▼▼▼▼▼▼

SYMPTOMS OF DEMON POSSESSION

Gleanings from *Demon Possession*, by Dr. F. L. Nevius

(1) The one under demon-power is an involuntary victim. (The willing soul is known as a medium.)

(2) The chief characteristic of demonomania is a distinct "other personality" within. (This is different to demon-influence, for in this men follow their own wills, and retain their own personality.)

(3) The demons have a longing for a body to possess (Matt. 12:43, 8:31), as it seems to give them some relief, and they enter the bodies of animals as well as men. There are distinctly individual peculiarities of the spirits.

(4) They converse through the organs of speech, and give evidence of personality, desire, fear.

(5) They give evidence of knowledge and power not possessed by the subject. In Germany, Pastor Blumhardt gives instances of demons speaking in all the European languages, and in some

languages unrecognizable. In France there were some cases having the "gift of tongues," speaking in German, Latin, Arabic.

(6) The demon in possession of the body entirely changes the moral character of those they enter, compelling them to act entirely contrary to their normal behavior. Reserved, reticent men will weep, sing, laugh, talk; meek souls will rage; ordinarily pure-tongued men and women will speak of things not to be named among children of God, and act in manner and conduct contrary to their normal dignity and behavior—all of which they are not responsible for while under "control" of this other personality within them. In brief, they will exhibit traits of character utterly different from those which belong to them normally.

(7) There are also nervous and muscular symptoms peculiar to demon possession in the body.

(8) There is also an afflatus of the breast, which is a special mark of demon possession.

(9) Oracular utterances are given in jerks and sentences, quite unlike the calm coherent sequence of language seen in the utterances of the apostles at Pentecost.

(10) There is "levitation" of the body—well known by spiritists—when the subject will say he is quite unconscious of possessing a body; and *there is invariably a passive mind.* There is often a distinct voice which speaks through the lips of the subject, expressing thoughts and words unintentionally.

▼▼▼▼▼▼▼▼

DEMONIACAL ACTIVITY IN LATER TIMES
From *Spirit Manifestations*, by Sir Robert Anderson

The Gospels testify to the activity of demons during the ministry of Christ on earth; and the Epistles warn us of a RENEWAL OF DEMONIACAL ACTIVITY in the "latter times," before His return. "All Scripture is God-breathed"; but it would seem that sometimes the revelation was made with special definiteness, and this particular warning is prefaced by the words: "the Spirit saith *expressly*." And it relates not to any new development of moral evil in the world, but to a new apostasy in the professing Church, a cult promoted by "seducing spirits" of a highly sensitive spirituality, and a more fastidious morality than Christianity itself will sanction (1 Tim. 4).

The Gospel narrative indicates that some demons were base and filthy spirits that exercized a brutalizing influence upon their victims. But the Lord plainly indicated that these were a class apart ("this kind," Mark 9:29). They were all "unclean spirits," but in Jewish use the word *akathartos* connoted *spiritual* defilement. That it did not imply moral pollution is proved by the fact that the Lord Jesus was charged with having a demon, though not even His most malignant enemies ever accused Him of moral evil. It was only by prayer that these filthy spirits could be cast out; whereas pious demons acknowledged Christ, and came out when His disciples commanded them to do so in His name. . . .

▼▼▼▼▼▼▼▼▼

THE PHYSIOLOGY OF THE SPIRIT
Gleanings from *Primeval Man Unveiled*, by James Gall

"The natural body has its senses, the spirit also has

its senses. . . ."

"There are busy senses within, examining and judging, approving and condemning, joying and grieving, hoping and fearing, after a fashion of their own, which no bodily sense can imitate. . . ."

"There is a spirit within which we call ourselves, and it is perfectly distinct from the body in which we dwell. . . ."

"If our spirits, which are generated in or with our bodies, are elaborated from immaterial substances into separate existences, constituting individual spirits, . . . these individual spirits must be presumed to be composed of spirit substance or substances, and possessed of different faculties. . . ."

"Our very language implies that the human spirit is an organism composed of parts mutually related, which, though individually different, are generically the same. . . ."

"It is a well established doctrine of Scripture, that the body is animated by an intelligent and immortal spirit, that feels and acts by means of its material mechanism, without being itself material. . . ."

▼▼▼▼▼▼▼▼▼

THE WORKING OF EVIL SPIRITS IN "CHRISTIAN" GATHERINGS

(1) SUPPOSED "CONVICTION OF SIN" BY DECEIVING SPIRITS

. . . I united with a number of brethren and sisters one whole week every month, in prayer to God to pour out more of His Spirit, gifts and power. After having done this for some time with great earnestness, such powerful and wonderful manifestations of God and His Holy Spirit (apparently) took place that we no longer doubted God had heard our prayer, and His Spirit had descended into our midst, and on our gathering. Amongst other things, this spirit, which we thought to be the Holy Spirit, used a fifteen-year-old girl as his instrument, through whom everyone belonging to our gathering, and having any sin or burden of conscience, had it revealed to the gathering. Nobody could remain in the meeting with any burden of conscience without it being revealed to the meeting by this spirit. For example: a gentleman of esteem and respect from the neighborhood came to the meeting, and all his sins were exposed in the presence of the gathering by the fifteen-year-old girl. Thereupon he took me into an adjoining room, so broken down, and admitted to me, with tears, that he had committed all these sins which the girl had exposed. He confessed this and all other sins known to him. Then he came again into the meeting, but hardly had he entered when the same voice said to him, "Ha! you have not confessed all yet; you have stolen ten gulden, that you have not confessed." In consequence, he took me again into the adjoining room and said, "It is true, I have also done this. . . ." This man had never seen this fifteen-year-old girl in his life, neither she him.

With such events, was it astonishing that a spirit of holy awe came over all at the meeting, and there was one controlling note which can only be expressed in the words, "Who among us shall dwell with the devouring fire? Who among us shall dwell with everlasting burnings? Fearfulness hath surprised the hypocrites." There was a most earnest spirit of adoration, and who could doubt when even the strong were broken down, and nobody dared remain in the meeting if they were a hindrance.

And yet we had to unmask this spirit which had brought about these things—and which we took to be the Holy Ghost—as a terrible power of darkness. I had such an uneasy feeling of distrust which could not be overcome. . . . As I made this known for the first time to an older brother and friend . . . he said, "Brother

Seitz, if you continue to foster unbelief, you can commit the sin against the Holy Ghost which will never be forgiven." These were terrible days and hours for me, because I did not know whether we had to do with the Power of God or a disguised spirit of Satan, and one thing only was clear to me, viz., that I and this meeting should not let ourselves be led by a spirit when we did not have clear light and confirmation whether this power was from above or below. Thereupon I took the leading brethren and sisters to the uppermost room of the house, and made known to them my position and said we must all cry and pray that we may be able to prove whether it was a power of light or darkness.

As we came downstairs the voice of this power said, using the fifteen-year-old girl as his instrument, "What is this rebellion in your midst? You will be sorely punished for your unbelief." I told this voice that it was true we did not know with whom we had dealings. But we wanted to be in that attitude, that if it was an angel of God, or the Spirit of God we would not sin against Him, but if it was a devil we would not be deceived by him. "If you are the power of God, you will be in accord as we handle the Word of God." "Try the spirits whether they be of God." We all knelt down and cried and prayed to God in such earnestness, that He would have mercy upon us, and reveal to us in some manner whom we had dealings with. Then the power had to reveal itself of its own accord. Through the person which he had been using as his instrument he made such abominable and terrible grimaces, and shrieked in such a piercing tone, "Now I am found out, now I am found out. . . ."

(2) SUPPOSED UNITY FOR "REVIVAL"

For some time now it has been on my mind to try to put into language some of the things which it has been my painful experience to witness, and pass through, in connection with the workings of Satan as an "angel of light," but everything seemed so complicated and confused. . . .

First: His attacks seem to be made upon the most spiritual souls—those who have made the fullest surrender to God, and who recognize a spiritual affinity which, they believe, if broken, mars the whole purpose of God (1 Cor. 1:10). The lying spirit insists on one mind, and judgment, and one expression. These souls thus "joined" form the "Assembly," so called, and claim Psalm 89:7. Everything is brought into the "Assembly" for decision, the assertion being that no individual soul can get the mind of the Lord, based on Proverbs 11:14, 5:22, and 20:18. Hours were spent in bringing the tiniest details of daily life before the Lord. The leader spread each matter, asking that all might be brought to one mind. The response was then given by each one in some word of Scripture. The attitude taken to receive the supposed "word of the Lord," was the RESISTANCE OF ANY THOUGHT OR REASON, and LETTING THE MIND BECOME A PERFECT BLANK. If anyone ventured to give an opinion—or any judgment—they were ruled out of fellowship; the fact of reasoning being the proof of the "flesh-life."

The discipline ministered to such was severe indeed. They were not allowed to speak to anyone, or to do any kind of work. In some cases this lasted for weeks, and even months. The effect upon the mind was very terrible. The only way back was by making a statement in the "Assembly" which satisfied them that there was true repentance. . . .

Proverbs 21:4 and Isaiah 59:3 are the words given for not working, and Romans 8:8. Prayer and reading the Word—all adds to sin; consequently the soul is shut up in torment and despair, being excluded from all meetings.

Second: The "manifestation of the Spirit" in prophecy, prayer and travail. One person would often pray for an hour, and sometimes two hours, without a break. Messages, too, would often last for two hours, and the whole meeting for eight or nine hours. Anyone yielding to sleep or exhaustion was at once pronounced "in the flesh," and a hindrance to the meeting.

"Travail" was manifested by tears, groans, and twisting of the body; and with some it was exactly like hysterics, and would last for hours. This was greatly encouraged as the means whereby God would work for the deliverance of souls—and those who did not come under this manifestation were judged as preserving their own life, not willing to "let go"—lovers of themselves; and it was believed that when the whole company were unitedly under the so-called "manifestation of the Spirit" then God would break through in revival. I might say here, that all this began with a nightly prayer meeting for revival, with no limit as to time.

The paralyzing fear of resisting God by any lack of submission, and evading the cross by an unwillingness to suffer, just sways the soul; and it dare not yield to one thought contrary to the "mind of Christ" in the "Assembly."

(3) SUPPOSED MANIFESTATIONS OF THE HOLY SPIRIT

From a book published in England in the early 1900's, said to contain the very words of the Lord Jesus, spoken THROUGH *some of His children, and written down as spoken in the first person, the following brief extract is taken, showing the extent of the mediumistic control by deceiving spirits, which by some are believed to be the work of the Holy Spirit.**

The Lord Jesus is supposed to have said:

"The manifestations of the Spirit, in some things, are very strange. Sometimes He will twist the body this way, and that, and the meaning is dark to you. I want

---

* This book is still circulating among deeply devoted believers, and is held by some as of equal value with the Bible.

you to know some things about this part of the Spirit's work. I want you to see that they are not useless.

"If you had spoken in your own tongue, when the Spirit came in, it would have graciously blessed you; but perhaps you might have thought it was *yourself*, as many have. So the Spirit comes in and speaks in an unknown tongue to you, that you might know that it was NOT YOURSELF SPEAKING.

"Your hands He has often lifted up, and again He has raised your fingers in various ways. Your eyes open and shut by the Spirit now, as they did not before. Your very head has been shaken by the Spirit and you have not known why He did this. You have thought, sometimes, it was just to show He was living there, and that is true, but there is more in it than that, and He will show you as well as He can, in a few words, what some of these things are. . . .

"Some things in the manifestations are very peculiar to you. You have gone on wondering about them. Don't think it strange that the Spirit works in you in many ways. His work is more than two-fold work. It is manifold. This is puzzling many minds. They see the Spirit shaking. They hear Him singing. They feel Him laughing, and they are sometimes tried with His various twistings and jerkings, as though He would tear them to pieces.

"Sometimes it seems He is imitating the animals in various sounds and doings. This has been all a mystery to the saints. His work, I say, is manifold. He seeks, in some, to show them that they are all one with each other, in the whole creation. . . . If He shows you, by making a noise as of some wild animal, that you are like that, you must not despise His way of working, for the Holy Spirit knows why He does it. He makes these noises in the animals, can't He make them in you?"

▼▼▼▼▼▼▼▼

LIGHT ON "ABNORMAL" EXPERIENCES*
Extract from a book published in Germany
by Pastor Ernst Lohmann
(Translated from the German)

Just as in a caricature the outstanding features of the true picture are to be found, so that a likeness is unmistakable, so phenomena which we find in heathen systems, in theosophy so-called, or new Buddhism, in spiritism, etc., resemble to some extent the divine manifestations called forth by the working of the Holy Spirit upon the spirit of man. They also produce revelations and prophecies, speaking and singing with tongues, healing and miracles. It is of importance that we should study this subject to find an answer to the question as to *how these phenomena are brought about.* It is self-evident that they are not manifestations of the Holy Spirit. The numerous and exact investigations which are being made in our day into the subject are giving us increasing insight into this dark realm. Powers and possibilities have been discovered in man, which until now have been totally unsuspected. They are designated "subliminal powers," and we speak of "subconsciousness."†

What physical occurrences accompany these phenomena? The lower nerve-centers (the ganglionic system, or the "vegetative" nerves, as they are called), which have their chief seat in the region round the pit

---

* From *The Overcomer* of 1920.

† J. Grasset, "Le Psychisme Infrérieur," 1906, writes: "Psychical proceedings fall into two groups: (1) those of a higher order—conscious, volitional, free; (2) those of a lower class—unconscious, mechanical, involuntary." On this subject Dr. Naum Kotik says in "The Emanation of Psycho-physical Energy": "Under ordinary conditions in the activity of the brain, the sub-consciousness hardly makes itself felt, and for this reason we have no suspicion of its existence. There

of the stomach, are excited to increased activity. At the same time the central region of the higher nervous system (the cerebral system), which in a normal state of affairs is the medium of conscious perception and action, becomes paralyzed. There is a reversal of the order of nature. The lower nerves take over the duty of the higher ones (a sort of compensation). This state of things comes to pass *negatively* by the higher organ losing its natural supremacy under pressure of illness, or artificially by hypnotism, auto-suggestion, etc.; and *positively* by the lower nerves being in some way *excited artificially* to increased activity, whereby they get the upper hand. These nerves then display abilities which our ordinary organs of sense do not possess; they receive impressions from a realm usually closed to us, such as clairvoyance, presentiments, prophecy, speaking with tongues, etc.

The Mohammedan soothsayer Dschalal-Ed-Dinrumi describes the trance-state as follows: "My eyes are closed and my heart is at the open gate." Anna Katharina Emmerich (1774–1824): "I see the light, not with my eyes, but it is as though I saw it with my *heart* (with the nerves which have their seat in the pit of the stomach) . . . that which is actually around me I see dimly with my eyes like one dozing and beginning to dream; my second sight is drawing me forcibly, and is clearer than my natural sight, but it does not take place through my eyes. . . ." When in a state of somnambulism, the inner sense, heightened in its activity, perceives outward things as clearly and more

---

are conditions of the psyche, however, such as somnambulism, in which the sub-consciousness comes to the front, takes over the complete control, and forces the super-consciousness back into the position in which it (viz., the sub-consciousness) rightfully belongs. The actions which attest the activity of the sub-consciousness independently of the super-consciousness are usually termed automatic."

so than when awake, when it recognizes tangible objects with eyes tightly closed and absolutely unable to see, just as well as by sight; this takes place, according to the unanimous declaration of all somnambulists, through the pit of the stomach, *i.e.*, through the nerves, which have their seat in this region. . . . And it is from this part that the nerves are set in action which move the organs of speech (in speaking with tongues, etc.). . . .

Numberless cases of false mysticism through all the centuries of Church history display the same characteristics, the subconsciousness being always the medium of such perception and functions. They are morbid, coming under the garb of divine manifestations to lead souls astray. Now, it is very significant that according to the assertions of the leaders, it is an activity of the *subconsciousness* that we meet with in the "Pentecostal Movement" (so-called). We read in a report of an "International Pentecostal Conference":

"On Tuesday, a pastor introduced the discussion. The main topic was the working of the subconscious mind in messages and prophecy. Much confusion prevailed concerning the relation of our consciousness to our subconsciousness. The scriptural discrimination was preferable (1 Cor. 14:14–15), where they were spoken of as 'understanding' and 'spirit.'

"When Christ lives in us He lives in our hearts, and in the heart are two chambers. In one room lives the conscience, and through the conscience I can know that Christ lives in me. In the other room of my heart there is the subconsciousness, and there also Christ lives. We look at 1 Corinthians 14:14, 'For if I pray in a tongue, my spirit prayeth, but my understanding is unfruitful.'"

Notice the expression "my spirit" (my subconscious mind), and also the expression "my understanding," *i.e.*, "When my spirit prays in tongues, my *subconscious mind* prays"!

In the Declaration of the Second Mulheim "Pentecostal Conference," September 15th, 1909, we read:

"In 1 Corinthians 14:14 (Luther's translation) Paul makes a distinction between the understanding and the spirit of man. By the word 'understanding' he means the conscious, and by the word 'spirit' the unconscious spiritual life, life of man. In this *unconscious* spiritual life—in modern language also termed 'subconsciousness'—God has placed the gift of speaking with tongues and prophecy. . . ."

According to this, *the spiritual life of the believer is synonymous with the subconsciousness of the somnambulist.* And the more highly developed this subconsciousness is in any individual, the more highly developed would be their spiritual life. Just try substituting the word "subconsciousness" in those passages where the Scripture speaks of the spirit of man; for example, Psalm 51:17, Psalm 77:6, Isaiah 66:2, Acts 7:59, Acts 18:5, Acts 20:22, Romans 1:9, Romans 2:29, Romans 8:16, 1 Corinthians 2:11, 1 Corinthians 4:21, 1 Corinthians 5:5, Galatians 6:1, Galatians 6:18, Ephesians 4:23, 1 Thessalonians 5:23.

Those in whom the subconsciousness becomes active in the manner described above, feel as it were an electric stream passing through the body, which is an *exciting of the nerves*, which have their central seat in the pit of the stomach. It is from thence that the jaws are moved in speaking with tongues.

One of the leaders of the "Pentecostal Movement," in describing the process of this so-called Baptism of the Spirit in his body, made use of the singular comparison that it seemed to him as though there were in his body an inverted bottle. The simile was incomprehensible to me, but this way of expressing it was most strikingly illuminated when I find an almost identical expression used by a Mohammedan soothsayer. Tewekkul Beg, a pupil of Mollah Schah, was receiving instruction from his master as to how he could get into the ecstatic state. He says: "After he had bound my eyes . . . I saw something in my inner being resembling a fallen tumbler. . . . When this object was placed upright a feeling of limitless bliss filled my being."

This feeling of bliss is another characteristic feature of this class of occurrences. By exciting the lower nervous system a feeling of intense rapture is regularly produced. . . . At first we find connected with it, usually, involuntary contraction of the muscles and movement of the limbs, in consequence of the unnatural inversion of the nervous system.

Pastor Paul again says:

"If anyone is to prophesy in the way I have now learned, God must be able to move the mouth of the one prophesying, as He formerly moved the mouth of Balaam's ass. The ass understood nothing of the words which she spoke, she only said what she was to say. There is a danger in uttering things we understand. It is so easy to mix in one's own thoughts, and then to utter what one thinks. This occurs without our intending it in the least. That is the reason why God trains His prophets in so preparing them that they utter exactly what the Spirit gives them. Speaking in strange tongues is a good preliminary school.

"There one learns to speak as the mouth is moved. One speaks without knowing what one is saying by simply following the position of the mouth. Just so in prophecy; there, too, one speaks as led by the position of the mouth. Speaking with tongues and prophesying are both on the same principle."

It is evident that in these phenomena we have the exact opposite of what the Scriptures understand by the communication of the Spirit. When the Spirit of God takes possession of the spirit of man, HE IS BROUGHT BACK TO A NORMAL CONDITION; the spirit acquires the full authority given it by the Creator over the powers of the soul, and through the soul over the body. The conscious personal life is once more completely under the authority of the spirit. The dependency upon God, which man sought to break off in his mania for exalting himself by setting his reason, his emotions, or the flesh upon the throne, is restored again. The Spirit of God can exercise once more His controlling and quickening power. The deeds of the flesh are put to death by the Spirit, the powers and the gifts of the Spirit developed, the man becomes spiritual, full of the Holy Spirit.

Note by Mrs. Penn-Lewis

The light given by Herr Lohmann will open the eyes of many perplexed believers, and give them intelligent understanding of much that has distressed them, and caused painful division among the most devoted children of God. It will also confirm the statements we have made concerning the working of evil spirits within the sphere of a believer, at the very same time that—up to the extent of his consciousness—he may know nothing against himself before the Lord; for Satan and his emissaries are well aware of the laws of the human frame and work along their line, arousing and exciting the natural life under the guise of its being spiritual.

The false conception of "surrender" as yielding the body to supernatural power, with the mind ceasing to act, is the highest subtlety of the enemy, and is exposed as such in this book, for it brings about—as Herr Lohmann explains—the paralysis of the "cerebral" systems, *i.e.*, the action of the mind, and allows the "vegetative nerves" full control and activity, excited by evil spirits. For the Holy Spirit dwells in and *acts through the spirit* of man, and not through either nerve center, which have both to be under the control of the spirit.

We have also pointed out again and again that "claiming the blood" cannot protect us from the enemy if in any way he is given ground, *e.g.*, if the cerebral nerves cease to act by "letting the mind go blank" (!) and the vegetative nerves are awakened to act in their place, so that the latter are excited to give "thrills" and "streams of life" through the body. No claiming of the precious blood of Christ will prevent these physical laws acting when the conditions for action are fulfilled. Hence, the strange fact which has perplexed many, that abnormal experiences manifestly contrary to the Spirit of God have taken place while the person was earnestly repeating words about the "blood."

Moreover, the arousing of the "vegetative nerves" to such abnormal activity that "floods of life" have appeared to pour through the whole body—the enemy whispering at the same moment, "This is divine!"—(1) dulls the mind and makes it inert in action, (2) causes a craving in the recipient for more of this "divine" life, (3) leads to the danger of ministration of it to others, and all that follows, as this path is pursued in honest faith and confidence of being "specially advanced" in the life of God.

Should any who are reading this discover their own case depicted, let them thank God for knowledge of the truth, and (1) simply reject by an attitude of will all that is not of God; (2) consent to trust God in His Word without any "experiences"; (3) stand on Romans 6:11, with James 4:7, in respect to the Adversary, and on John 16:13 in respect to the Holy Spirit.

▼▼▼▼▼▼▼▼▼

How Demons Attack Advanced Believers

Extracts from an article contributed to an American paper and reprinted in *The Christian* some years ago. We do not know the writer's name.

(1) The manifestation of demon power

The agency of demons is always brought more conspicuously into notice when God also is at work, in proportion to the manifestation and power of God's work among souls. When the Son of God was manifest in the flesh, it called forth the activity and outspoken agency of demons more than ever before.

(2) Various kinds of demons

Demons are of a multiplied variety. They are of various types, greater in diversity than human beings, and these demons always seek to possess a person congenial to them in some characteristic. The Bible tells us of unclean demons, of fortune-telling demons, of despotic demons, theological demons, screeching and yelling demons. There are demons that act particularly on the body, or some organ or appetite of the body. There are others that act more directly upon the intellect, or the sensibilities, and emotions and affections. There are others of a higher order that act directly on man's spiritual nature, upon the conscience or the spiritual perceptions. These are the ones that act as angels of light, and sidetrack and delude many who are real Christians.

(3) How demons fasten on human beings

They seek out those whose make-up and temperament is most congenial to themselves, and then seek to fasten themselves on to some part of the body, or brain, or some appetite, or some faculty of the mind—either the reason, or imagination, or perception; and when they get access, they bury themselves into the very structure of the person, so as to identify themselves with the personality of the one they possess. In a great many instances they do not get possession of the individual, but obtain such a hold on some part of the mind as to torment the person with periodical attacks of something strange and abnormal, out of all proportion to the general character and make-up of the individual.

(4) THE OBJECT OF DEMONS SEEKING HUMAN BEINGS

These demons feed themselves on the person with whom they are allied. . . . There are allusions in Scripture, and facts gathered from experience, sufficient to prove that certain varieties of demons live on the juices in human blood. . . .

(5) THE CLASS OF DEMONS WHICH ATTACK ADVANCED CHRISTIANS

There are religious demons, not holy, but nevertheless religious, and filled with a devilish form of religion which is the counterfeit of true, deep spirituality. These pseudo-religious demons very rarely attack young beginners, but they hover around persons who *advance into deeper experiences*, and seek every opportunity to fasten themselves upon the conscience, or the spiritual emotions of persons of high states of grace, and especially if they are of a vivid or energetic temperament. These are the demons that play havoc among many professors of holiness. One way they get hold of persons is as follows: A soul goes through a great struggle, and is wonderfully blessed. Floods of light and emotion sweep through the being. *The shore lines are all cut.* The soul is launched out into a sea of extravagant experience. At such a juncture these demons hover round the soul, and make strange suggestions to the mind of something odd, or outlandish, or contrary to common sense or decent taste. They make these suggestions under the profession of being the Holy Ghost. They fan the emotions, and produce a strange, fictitious exhilaration, which is *simply their bait to get into some faculty of the soul. . . .*

(6) Some examples of how demons take hold of apparently Spirit-filled Christians

A very holy and useful woman says that soon after receiving the baptism of the Spirit, there came to her one night in the church a wild, abnormal impulse to throw the hymnbook at the preacher, and run all over the church screaming; and it took all her will power to keep her hand from throwing that book. But she had common sense to know that the Holy Spirit was not the author of such a suggestion. If she had yielded to that sudden feeling, it would have likely given that fanatical demon admission to her emotional nature and ruined her life-work. She is a person who knows the mighty demonstrations of the Holy Spirit, and understands God sufficiently to know He is not the source of wild and indecent conduct. . . .

Another person said he felt like rolling on the floor, and groaning and pulling the chairs around, but he distinctly perceived that the impulse to do so had something wild in it, and a touch of self-display contrary to the gentleness and sweetness of Jesus; and, as quick as he saw it was an attack of a false spirit, he was delivered. But another man had the same impulse, and fell down groaning and roaring, beating the floor with his hands and feet, and the demon entered into him as the angel of light, and got him to think that his conduct was of the Holy Ghost; and it became a regular habit in the meetings he attended, until he would ruin every religious meeting he was in. . . .

(7) The most dangerous class of demons

It requires great humility to try these spirits and detect the false ones. Other demons in existence are those pseudo-pious ones who *soar round the high altitudes of the spiritual life*, like eagles around great mountain tops, and seek to fasten their talons upon the lofty and conspicuous prey. These are the demons of spiritual pride, of religious ambition, of false prophetic vision, of strained and far-fetched illuminations, of wild fantastic notions. These are the demons that flit over the sunlit regions in the land of Canaan, and attack very seldom any but *advanced believers.*

(8) Some effects of demon influence

The effects of being influenced by this sort of demons are manifold, and plainly legible to a well-poised mind. They cause people to run off into things that are odd and foolish, unreasonable and indecent. It leads them to adopt a peculiar voice or twang, or unnatural shouting, or some shaking of the body; or such an influence is manifested by peculiar heresies in the mind, of which there is a nameless variety. It produces a certain wildness in the eye and harshness in the voice. Such persons invariably break the law of love, and *severely condemn people who do not conform to themselves.* As a rule such persons lose their flesh, for demoniac possession is very wearing on the vital forces and produces a terrible strain on the heart and nervous system.

THE TRUE WORKINGS OF GOD, AND COUNTERFEITS OF SATAN

"I pray that your love may abound yet more and more in knowledge and all discernment: so that ye may distinguish the things that differ, that ye may be sincere and void of offence . . ." (Phil. 1:9–10, mg.)

True	Counterfeit
1. *The Baptism or Fullness of the Spirit:* Is a true baptizing into the Body of Christ and into oneness with all the members of the Body. Its special mark and result is known in power to witness for Christ, and in conviction of sin in others and their turning to God. The highest manifestation of the Fullness of the Spirit is coexistent with the use of the faculties and self-control. There is but one reception of the Holy Spirit—with many succeeding experiences, developments, or new crises, resultant on fresh acts of faith or apprehension of truth; individual believers have varied degrees of the same Infilling of the Spirit, according to specific conditions. The enduement of power for service is often a definite experience in many lives.	1. Counterfeit workings of evil spirits may accompany a true reception of the Fullness of the Holy Spirit, if the believer "lets go" his mind into "blankness" and yields his body up passively to supernatural power. As a "blank mind" and "passive body" is contrary to the condition for use required by the Holy Spirit, and is the primary condition necessary for evil spirits to work, the anomaly is found in the Holy Spirit responding to the law of faith, and filling the man's spirit, at the same time that evil supernatural powers respond to the law of passivity fulfilled in mind and body. They then can produce in the senses manifestations which seem to be the outcome of the Holy Spirit's entry to the spirit. The results of the counterfeit manifestations are varied, and wide in their ramifications, according to specific conditions. The abstract result is great "manifestations" with little real fruit; a spirit of division from others, instead of unity, etc., etc.
2. *The presence of God:* Known in and by the human spirit,	2. The counterfeit of the presence of God is mainly felt upon

True	Counterfeit
through the Holy Spirit. When He fills the atmosphere of a room, the *spirit* of the man is conscious of it, not his senses. The faculties of those present are alert and clear and they retain freedom of action. The spirit is made tender (Ps. 34:18), and the will pliable to the will of God. All the actions of a person moved by the true and pure presence of God are in accord with the highest ideal of harmony and grace.	the body, and by the physical senses, in conscious "fire," "thrills," etc. The counterfeit of the "presence" in the atmosphere is felt by the senses of the body, as "breath," "wind," etc., while the mind is passive or inactive. The person affected by this counterfeit "presence" will be moved almost automatically to actions he would not perform of his own will and with all his faculties in operation. He may not even remember what he has done when under the "power" of this "presence," just as a sleepwalker knows nothing of his actions when in that state. The inaction of the mind can often be seen by the vacant look in the eyes.
3. *God in and with man in the spirit:* John 14:23. The Father in heaven is realized to be a real Father (Gal. 4:6), the Son a real Saviour, the Holy Spirit a real Person; manifested as One in the spirit of the believer, by the Holy Spirit: with resulting effects as in Romans 8:9 to 11.	3. Evil spirits counterfeit, as the occasion serves them, each Person of the Trinity, and can thus produce manifestatations given to the senses in which the real spirit-sense may have no part.
4. *Christ manifested* in the believer by His Spirit, so that He is known as a Living Person on the Throne in heaven, and the believer joined in spirit to Him there, with the result that Christ's life and nature is imparted to him, forming and building up in him a "new creation" (Gal. 1:16, 4:19, Col. 1:27), the believer growing up into Him in	4. Christ apparently manifested inwardly as a "Person," to whom the soul prays, or with whom he holds communion, yet there is no real evidence of the expression of the divine nature or a true growth of the Christ life, with a deepening fellowship with the Christ in heaven. On the contrary, the Christ in heaven seems far away. The counterfeit centers

True	Counterfeit
all things.*	and ends in an "experience" which keep the person introverted or self-centered (spiritually).
5. *Consciousness of God:* Felt in the spirit, and not by the physical senses.	5. "Consciousness" of "God" in bodily sensations, which feed the "flesh" and overpower the true spirit-sense.
6. *The holiness of God:* When realized by the believer it produces worship and godly awe, with a hatred of sin. On the ground of the blood of Calvary, God draws near to men, seeking their love, and His presence does not terrorize.	6. Evil spirits counterfeit this by giving a terror of God, which drives men away from Him, or forces them into actions of slavish fear, apart from the use of the mind and will in glad, voluntary obedience to Him.
7. *Surrender to God:* Of spirit, soul and body, is a simple yielding or committal to Him of the whole man, to do His will and be at His service. God asks the full cooperation† of the man in the intelligent use of all his faculties (Rom. 6:13).	7. Passive yielding of spirit, soul and body to supernatural power, to be moved automatically, in passive, blind obedience, apart from the use of volition or mind. Evil spirits desire control of a man, and his passive submission to them.
8. *Fellowship with the sufferings of Christ:* The result of faithful witness for Him; and in such "suffering" the joy of the Spirit breaks forth in one's spirit (Acts 5:41). The fruit of true conformity to Christ's death in "the fellowship of His sufferings" is	8. Suffering caused by evil spirits is characterized by a fiendish acuteness, and is fruitless in result—the victim being hardened instead of mellowed by it. The demons can cause anguished suffering in spirit, soul or body. "Possession" manifested

* See "Counterfeit" for the difference between turning inward to a subjective manifestation and relying upon the Living Christ in heaven. The reliance and fellowship with the Glorified Christ draws the believer to live out of himself (Eph. 2:6), and thus have a wider vision, and clearer fellowship with all saints.

† "Cooperation" versus "control" is the distinction between the true working of God in and with men and the working of evil supernatural powers.

True	Counterfeit
seen in life to others, and growth in tenderness of spirit and Christ-likeness in character (2 Cor. 4:10–12).	in abnormal suffering may be the fruit of (unconscious) acceptance of sufferings caused by evil spirits, often under the name of "the will of God."
9. *Trusting God:* A true faith given of God in the spirit, having its origin in Him, reckoning without effort upon Him to fulfill His written Word. It coexists with the full use of every faculty in intelligent action. "Faith" is a fruit of the Spirit and cannot be forced. Gal. 5:22, 1 Cor. 13.	9. Trusting evil spirits comes about through trusting blindly some supernatural words, or revelations, supposed to come from God—which produces a forced "faith," or faith beyond the believer's true measure, the result being actions which lead into paths of trial never planned by God.
10. *Reliance upon God:* An attitude of the will, of trust and dependence upon God, taking Him at His word, and depending upon His character of faithfulness.	10. Reliance upon evil spirits means a passive leaning upon supernatural help and experience, which draws the person away from faith in God Himself, and from active co-action with Him.
11. *Communion with God:* fellowship in the Spirit with Christ in the glory as one spirit with Him. The consciousness of this is in the spirit (John 4:24) only, and not in "feelings" in the senses. See for conditions of true communion with God, 1 John 1:5–7.	11. Communion with evil spirits may take place by retiring within to enjoy sense communion in "exquisite feelings," which absorbs and renders the soul incapable of the duties of life. The "flesh" is fed by this spurious spiritual "communion" as really as in grosser ways.
12. *Waiting on God:* The spirit in restful cooperation with the Holy Spirit, awaiting God's time to act and to fulfill His promises. The true waiting upon God can be coexistent with the keenest activity of mind and service.	12. A "waiting for the Spirit to come," in hours of prayer, which brings those who "wait" into passivity—which at last reaches a point of "seance" conditions, followed by an influx of lying spirits in manifestations.
13. *Praying to God:* Having access to the Holiest of all, on the ground of the blood (Heb. 10:19). Penetrating in spirit through the	13. Praying to evil spirits comes about by praying to "God" in the atmosphere, or within, or possibly to "pictures" of God in

True	Counterfeit
lower heavens to the Throne of Grace (Heb. 4:14–16). True "prayer" is not directed toward God as within the believer, but to a Father in heaven, in the name of the Son, by the Holy Spirit.	the mind, instead of approaching the Throne of Grace according to Hebrews 10:19.
14. *Asking God:* An act of the will in simple faith, making a transaction with God in heaven on the ground of His written Word. "Answers to prayer" from God are usually so unsensational and so unobtrusive that the petitioner often does not recognize the answer.	14. "Asking" evil spirits, by speaking to some supernatural presence in or around the person. The "answers" are generally dramatic, sensational, calculated to over-awe the person, and make him feel he is a wonderful recipient of favor from on high.
15. *God speaking:* Through His Word, by His Spirit, in the spirit and conscience of the man, illuminating the mind to understand the will of the Lord.	15. Evil spirits speaking: either puffing up, accusing, condemning or confusing the person, so that he is bewildered or distracted and cannot exercise his reason or judgment. The "speaking" of accusing spirits resembles thinking or speaking to oneself, when the words are not uttered audibly.
16. *The voice of God:* Is heard and known in the spirit of man, wherein the Spirit of God dwells. God also speaks through the conscience, and through the written Word, never confusing or dulling the faculties of the man or perplexing him so as to hinder clearness of judgment and reason. The true voice of God does not make a demand of unreasoning obedience to it, irrespective of the man's free volition.	16. The counterfeit "voice" of God is usually loud and comes from outside the person. It is frequently imperative and persistent, urging sudden action. It is confusing and clamorous, or subtle in suggestion. It produces fear through its insistent demands, making the man a slave to supernatural power. It may also be distinguished from the voice of God by its sometimes trivial objective, and fruitless results when obeyed.
17. *Divine guidance:* Through the spirit and mind; *i.e.*, "drawing" in spirit, light in the mind:	17. Satanic guidance by supernatural voices, visions, leadings, drawings, are all de-

True	Counterfeit
spirit and mind brought into one accord in harmony with the principles of the Word of God (Eph. 5:17; Phil. 1:9–11).	pendent upon the passivity of the mind and reason, and take place in the sense-realm as a counterfeit of the true in the spirit.
18. *Divine "leadings":* Are in the spirit; demand cooperation of the man in every faculty of mind and spiritual intelligence in correctly reading the monitions of the Spirit. The will is always left free to choose and act. The true "leading of the Spirit" is never out of accord with principles of God's Word.	18. Satanic "leadings" and impulses demand passive surrender of mind and body. They are compulsory in effect, and all "compelling" and "compulsion" from the supernatural realm indicates the work of deceiving spirits.
19. *Divine "visions":* When given, come (1) without seeking for them, (2) with definite purpose, (3) are never abortive, and (4) are coexistent with active use of the mind and faculties.	19. Satanic visions (1) demand a passive state, (2) are broken by mental action, (3) are frequently contrary to truth, and (4) fruitless in result. They destroy all faith-reliance on God.
20. *Obedience to God:* An act of deliberate will, choosing to do the will of God when it is made known to the believer. A full examination of the source of the command before deciding to obey is consistent with true obedience.	20. The counterfeit of "obedience" is a passive, automatic, blind yielding to supernatural power or voices, apart from intelligent apprehension of results or consequences. The person fears to question or examine the source of the command.
21. *God giving power:* By the Holy Spirit in the man's spirit, strengthening him in spirit, so as to energize his mind and every faculty of his being to their fullest use, and enabling him to endure and accomplish what he could not bear or do apart from God (Eph. 3:16).	21. Evil spirits give power in a supernatural energy—generally spasmodic and unreliable—dependent upon the man being passive in spirit, soul and body. This "power," when it ceases, leaves the man dull and exhausted, the effect generally being attributed to natural causes.
22. *God giving influence:* Means that the believer draws others to God, not to himself. True divine "influence" does not "control" others automatically,	22. Evil spirits giving "influence" means a control or power over others which causes them to act apart from their volition or reason. This "power" may be ex-

True	Counterfeit
but constrains them to turn to God.	ercised unknowingly by persons the demons can use in this way.
23. *God giving "impressions":* Means a gentle movement in the spirit, which leaves the person free to act of his own volition, and does not compel him to action. "Impressions from God" are within—in the shrine of the spirit—and not from a "power" outside, *e.g.*, in "touches" on the body, or an exterior compelling force.	23. Evil spirits' "impressions" are from outside, upon the person, and require certain conditions for the "impressions" to be given—*i.e.*, a sitting still and waiting, etc. These conditions can also be fulfilled unconsciously by cultivating passivity of the whole being.
24. *Divine life from God:* Is known not by "consciousness" but by results, enabling the believer to bear and suffer what he could not bear or suffer humanly. There is rarely any "feeling" of strength or life, because consciousness of divine life would draw the man from the path of faith to rely upon his experience.	24. "Life" in thrills, etc., given by evil spirits, is known by its being in the senses, giving pleasant sensations rather than true power. When it passes away, the person is dulled or weakened, and may go into spiritual darkness through numbness of the sensibilities; *e.g.*, he says he is "like a stone."
25. *Divine love:* Shed abroad in the heart by the Holy Spirit, is coexistent with keen and faithful dealing with sin; with acute hatred to sin and Satan, and all that is contrary to righteousness. God's love does not dull, but energizes every faculty to fulfill the action for which it was intended in creation. It has no "craving" in it, nor does it weaken those to whom it flows out.	25. Counterfeit of the "love of God" makes the recipient cover over sin, compromise with it; dulls him to keen-edged righteousness; makes him incapable of true hatred to the things that God hates, for the faculty which "loves" is also the faculty which hates. The counterfeit of love, whether human or divine, given by evil spirits, grips the sensibilities with an overmastering and painful "craving" for its object.
26. *Fire from God:* Is a purifying through suffering (Matt. 3:11–12), or a consuming zeal in spirit, which deepens into white heat intensity to do the will and	26. "Fire" caused by evil spirits is generally a glow in the body, which the believer thinks is a manifestation of "God" in "possession" of the body, but after-

True	Counterfeit
work of God, which no trials or opposition can quench. Fire from God is spiritual, not literal, and therefore falls upon the spirit, not the body.	wards results in darkness, dullness and weakness with no reasonable cause; or else it continues deceiving the believer into counterfeit experiences.
27. *Texts from God:* These are given through the organ of the spirit to the mind, when the spirit is (1) calm, (2) unstrained, (3) at liberty, (4) open to the Spirit of God. They do not confuse, and when acted upon are found to be confirmed in the situation, and are always in accord with the keen use of the faculties. Intelligent knowledge of the broad principles of Scripture is needed for the true interpretation of "texts" which arise in the spirit, lest they be misused through human conceptions of divine things, *e.g.*, the mind may take literally what God means spiritually.	27. Texts from evil spirits "flash" into the mind—rush in with force; come from without, sometimes audibly. They elate or crush, condemn or puff up; confuse or turn out fruitless, leading those who obey them into vain actions, or into wreckage of circumstances. Evil spirits give a false "experience" and then "texts to confirm it," whereas a true experience confirms the truth of the statements of the written Word. Evil spirits make use of all misconceptions of truth.
28. *Sin from the fallen nature:* Is from within, carries the will with it, or else forces the will by its pressure. The man knows the movement to sin is sin, and yet yields to it. Romans 6:6, 11 and 12 is God's way of dealing with the fallen nature and its workings, as the believer stands on the ground of the cross, and wields Christ's finished Calvary work as a weapon for victory. The Holy Spirit bears witness to the cross in setting us free from sin when it is a fruit of the evil nature.	28. Sin caused by evil spirits—apart from temptation—is also from within, but is forced into the spirit, mind or body against the desire of the man, and should be recognized as distinctly *not* of or from himself, *e.g.*, blasphemous thoughts and unexplainable "feelings." If the "sin" infused by demons is dealt with as from the evil nature, even though the person stands on Romans 6 and refuses it, no deliverance comes; but when it is recognized as the work of demons, and resisted on the ground of the cross, freedom is quickly given.
29. *Self-examination in the light of God:* A thoughtful analy-	29. Self-introspection, which is made use of by evil spirits to

True	Counterfeit
sis of his own actions exercised by the spiritual man, which does not produce "despair," "disappointment," a "crushed feeling," etc., but leads to rapid decision of action, and a joyous faith in the cooperating work of the Spirit in deliverance from all that does not bear the verdict of the light of God (John 3:21).	throw the believer into self-accusation and despair. This drives the person inward and downward to crushed impotence and faithlessness. God never crushes His children. He convicts only to reveal the remedy. Evil spirits seek to turn souls to self-centered absorption, whereas God moves in them to live and care for others.
30. *Conviction of sin:* Comes to the conscience from the Word of God, or by the direct action of the Holy Spirit, in times of quiet prayer or reading. It is never "vague" or confusing, and ceases as soon as the man decides to obey the Word or go to God for cleansing in the blood of Christ. True conviction is also a deepening experience as the light of God shines into the conscience and life.	30. Evil spirits' accusations, which are a counterfeit of conviction, are from without, in the ear (audibly) or to the mind, in a "nagging," persistent, confusing kind of "speaking," often without definite purpose or specific reason. No "confessing" or "step of obedience" affects these accusations, and they come again and again over the same things. Many live under a perpetual cloud through the attacks of accusing spirits. They are under the shadow of being "always wrong."
31. *Confession of sin:* Whether to God or man, it should be a deliberate act of the will in obedience to the Word of God and one's conscience. It should be followed by sincere repentance and a putting away of the confessed sin. It will have the witness of the Spirit to the conscience that the sin has been put away through the efficacy of the blood of Christ.	31. Compulsory confessions, forced by the driving power of evil spirits upon the mind in accusation, or from remorse. To silence the accusing voices the man is sometimes impelled to confess "sins" which have no actual existence.

True	Counterfeit

Notes (True)

Without exception, the manifestation of the Holy Spirit is marked by (1) a Christ-like spirit of love, (2) soberness of spirit vision, (3) keenness of vision, (4) deep humility of heart and meekness of spirit, with lion-courage against sin and Satan, and (5) clearness of the mental faculties with a "sound mind" (2 Timothy 1:7).

"Wherefore be ye not foolish, but understand what the will of the Lord is . . ." (Eph. 5:17).

Notes (Counterfeit)

Speaking generally, proof that manifestations are "sense-manifestations" from deceiving spirits may be found in the attitude being wrong, *e.g.*, (1) A condemning and judging spirit; (2) the spirit-vision is dulled; one cannot see marks of God at work in other ways; (3) an absence of true Spirit-power in (*a*) conviction of sin, (*b*) deliverance of souls, or (*c*) salvation of souls; or (4) the spirit is "sweet" in a weak sense, with mind dulled, and unable to work with clearness.

This book was produced by the Christian Literature Crusade. We hope it has been helpful to you in living the Christian life. CLC is a literature mission with ministry in over 45 countries worldwide. If you would like to know more about us, or are interested in opportunities to serve with a faith mission, we invite you to write to:

Christian Literature Crusade
P.O.Box 1449
Fort Washington, PA 19034